1978

PEOPLES OF THE EARTH

volume	1	Australia and Melanesia (including New Guinea)
volume	2	Africa from the Sahara to the Zambesi
volume	3	Europe (including USSR west of the Urals)
volume	4	Mexico and Central America
volume	5	Islands of the Atlantic (including the Caribbean)
volume	6	Amazonia, Orinoco and pampas
volume	7	Andes
volume	8	The Pacific – Polynesia and Micronesia
volume	9	Southern Africa and Madagascar
volume	10	Indonesia, Philippines and Malaysia
volume	11	South-East Asia
volume	12	The Indian subcontinent (including Ceylon)
volume	13	China (including Tibet), Japan and Korea
volume	14	USSR east of the Urals
volume	15	Western and central Asia
volume	16	The Arctic
volume	**17**	**The Arab World**
volume	18	North America
volume	19	Man the craftsman
volume	20	The Future of Mankind. General Index

volume seventeen

The Arab World

THE DANBURY PRESS

(Preceding page) The desert sands of Arabia have stirred a romantic chord in the western soul. In many ways little has changed – the word of the prophet still rules the lives of fierce tribesmen and liquid eyed women mysteriously secluded behind their veils. But in the last few decades oil has thrust the Arabian world into the 20th century and now one is as likely to see a city of skyscrapers as Beduin tents, or a Cadillac crossing the desert beside a caravan of camels.

Contents

Supervisory Editor of the Series:
Professor Sir Edward Evans-Pritchard,
Fellow of All Souls, Professor of Social Anthropology,
University of Oxford, 1946-1970,
Chevalier de la Légion d'Honneur

Volume Editor:
Dr Ahmed Al-Shahi,
St Antony's College, University of Oxford

The Danbury Press
a division of Grolier Enterprises Inc.

Publisher
ROBERT B. CLARKE

Library of Congress Catalog Card No. 72 85614

Printed in Italy by
Arnoldo Mondadori Editore, Verona

STAFF CREDITS
Editorial Director **Tom Stacey**
Picture Director **Alexander Low**
Executive Editor **Katherine Ivens**
Art Director **Tom Deas**
Assistant Editor **Elisabeth Meakin**
Project Co-ordinator **Anne Harrison**
Research **Cheryl Moyer**

Specialist Picture Research **Elly Beintema**
Picture Research **Claire Baines/Diana Eggitt**
Jeanne Griffiths/Carolyn Keay/Emma Stacey
Editorial Assistants **Richard Carlisle/Rosamund Ellis**
Mira Bar-Hillel/Susan Rutherford/Pamela Tubby
Editorial Secretary **Caroline Silverman**
Design Assistants **Susan Forster**
Richard Kelly
Cartography **Ron Hayward**
Illustrations **Sandra Archibald, Ron McTrusty**

Production **Roger Multon**
Production Editor **Vanessa Charles**

The publishers gratefully acknowledge help from the following organizations:
Royal Anthropological Institute, London
Musée de l'Homme, Paris
International African Institute, London
British Museum, London
Royal Geographical Society, London
Scott Polar Research Institute, Cambridge
Royal Asiatic Society, London
Royal Central Asian Society, London
Pitt-Rivers Museum, Oxford
Horniman Museum, London
Institute of Latin American Studies, London

PICTURE CREDITS
Cover: **Eve Arnold, Micha Bar-Am** (both from the John Hillelson Agency), **Victor Englebert. Roger Akester** 80 through 83. **Ardea Photographics** 130 r. **Marc and Evelyne Bernheim** (Woodfin Camp) 92 – 93, 100 c & bl, 101. **Mehmet Biber** 17 t. **John Bulmer** 55 l & br. **Peter Carmichael** (C.S.M. Pictures) 90 bl. **Michael Cox** 29. **Tor Eigeland** (Black Star, New York) 76 b. **Victor Englebert** 94 through 99, 100 t, 108 through 117. **Robert Freson** (Peter Schub) 13 br, 36. **Garofalo** (Paris Match) 107. **Pascal Grellety-Bosniel** (C.I.R.I.) 68 r. **Sonia Halliday** 13 bl, 89 tr, 91 b. From the John Hillelson Agency – **Eve Arnold** 20 tl, 22 – 23, 24, 25 br, 26, 63 br, 64, 65, 66 r, 67 r, 68 l, 73, 74 r, 75 r, 76 tl, 79, **Micha Bar-Am** 38 – 39, 40 bl, 41, 42 t, 43, 46 c & bl, 48 exc br, **Georg Gerster** 56, **Burt Glinn** 123 br, **David Hurn** 128 bl & r, **George Rodger** 2 – 3, 102 – 103, 104 exc tr, 105. Gamma from the John Hillelson Agency – **Raymond Depardon** 106 tl, **Christian Simonpietri** 21 t, 34 cr, 62, 78 br. Magnum from the John Hillelson Agency – **Bruno Barbey** 18 – 19, 20 bl, 21 br & l, 25 tr, 50 through 54, 55 tr, 57 bl, 63 l, 106 b, 124, 125, 130 l, 131, 133 cr, **Ian Berry** 42 bl, 121 br, 133 br, **Brian Brake** 70 – 71, 78 t & bl, **René Burri** 47, 66 l, 72, 75 bl, **Charles Harbutt** 44 – 45, 46 r, **Marc Riboud** 118 – 119, 120, 121 tl, 122, 123 t, 126, 127, 128 t, 129. **Peter Keen** (Daily Telegraph) 13 t & cl. **Alexander Low** (Daily Telegraph) 13 tr. **Melet** (Paris Match) 104 tr. **Christian Monty** 59, 84. **S. Pandis** 17 b. **Paris Match** 106 tr. **Angelo Pesce** (Kabao) 14. **Paul Popper** 17 br. **Folco Quilici** (Moana) 37, 60 – 61, 88. **Peter Schub** 31, 32, 33, 34 bl & tr, 35, 63 tr. **Ted Spiegel** 40 t, 48 br. **Sabine Weiss** (Rapho, New York) 86 – 87, 89 tl & br, 90 t, 91 t. **Nik Wheeler** (Black Star, New York) 57 t & cr, 67 l, 69. **E. Zalka** 77.
Key: **t**=top, **c**=center, **b**=bottom, **r**=right, **l**=left.

Peoples of the Earth, volumes one to twenty

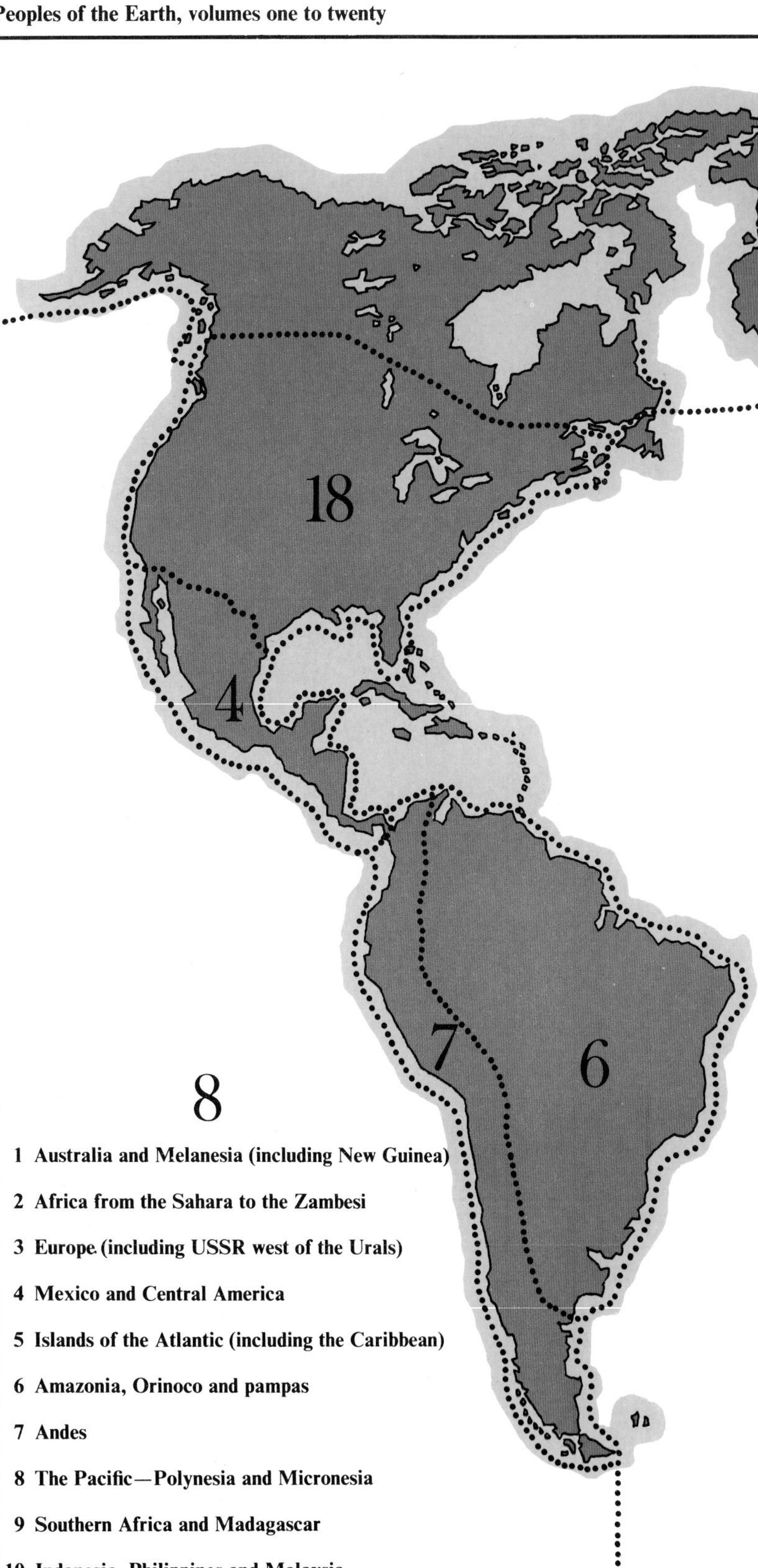

1 Australia and Melanesia (including New Guinea)
2 Africa from the Sahara to the Zambesi
3 Europe (including USSR west of the Urals)
4 Mexico and Central America
5 Islands of the Atlantic (including the Caribbean)
6 Amazonia, Orinoco and pampas
7 Andes
8 The Pacific—Polynesia and Micronesia
9 Southern Africa and Madagascar
10 Indonesia, Philippines and Malaysia

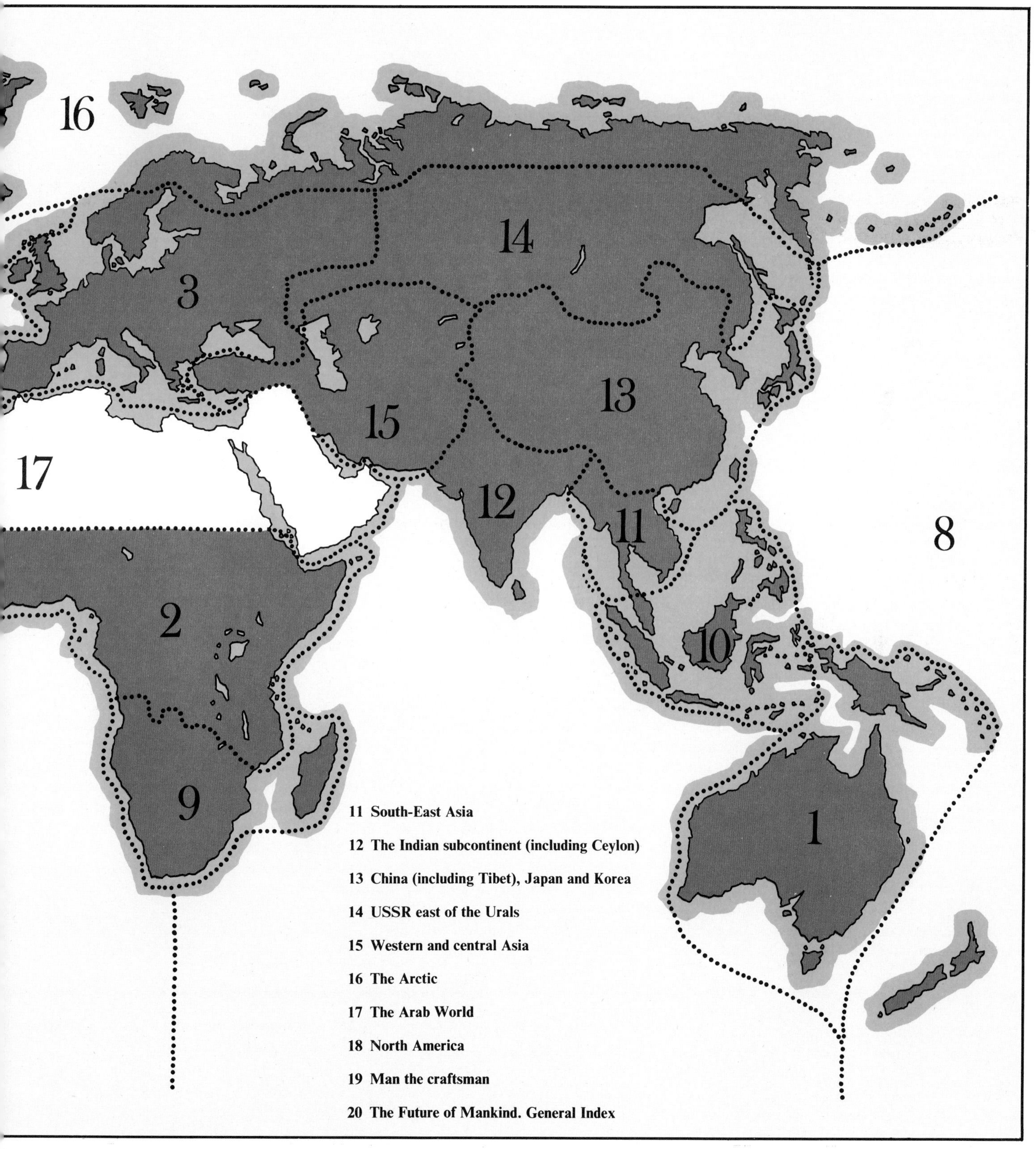

16
3
14
15
13
17
12
11
8
2
10
9
1

The meeting and mingling of races

'*What happens when peoples meet? Peoples are fascinating in themselves but equally interesting are the encounters between them and the kinds of adjustments which they make when they live together in the same country. Students of ethnic, cultural and race relations try to make systematic and meaningful studies of this whole important field.*'

Arnold Toynbee put one aspect of the total process very dramatically when he wrote that the great event of the 20th century is the impact of the western civilization upon all the other living societies of the world, an impact so powerful and pervasive that it has turned the lives of all its victims upside down and inside out, profoundly affecting their behavior, outlook, feelings and beliefs. 'New lives for old' is how another described the devastating effect of a million western soldiers upon a relatively untouched South Pacific island people during World War II.

Certainly the overseas expansion of western nations and states since the late 15th century is immensely significant and it provides one framework within which to examine the interaction of peoples and cultures in all continents. Portugal, Spain, Holland, Britain, France, Belgium, Germany, Denmark, Italy provided some of the principal navigators, explorers, prospectors, traders, slavers, conquerors, governors, settlers. The settlers, in turn, from their national bases in North America, South Africa and Australasia were also responsible for extending the western presence and influence.

Nevertheless it is necessary to bear in mind that the western impact has varied greatly in intensity. Some peoples, the Amerindians of North America, have been subjected to major incursions of western populations and technology, others, Papuans and New Guineans, southern Sudanese, or some remote Amazonians, have remained isolated and virtually unaffected although helicopters, space satellites and the like may now reduce the privacy of all. Again some civilizations or cultures, those of China and India are cases, have proved stronger or better-equipped to hold their own even when invaded.

An important consequence of widespread domination has been the transportation of substantial populations of slaves, indentured and other laborers: Africans to the Caribbean and the Americas, Indians to Fiji, East and South Africa, Trinidad and Guyana. In no instance have those transported been exactly similar even when drawn from the same areas. African, Indian and Chinese migrants have reflected the many different languages, religions, castes, tribes, the sub-cultures as well as the cultures, of the continents or sub-continents from which they were drawn. Variety has also marked the European deportees, refugees and settlers through the centuries. Puritans in New England; in Barbados, post Civil War royalists from Cornwall in England; convicts in Tasmania; Breton, Moravian and Hutterite communities in Canada; Irish in New South Wales; Scots in the south of New Zealand; Russian Jews, German Jews, French Huguenots, Ukrainians, Orthodox and Catholic . . . All provide reminders of diversity, and of history, including the history of human conflict and persecution. The colorful patchwork of peoples throughout the present-day world owes much to such prolonged ethnic interweaving during the era of western overlordship.

Patchwork is an appropriate description for the peoples of the world whether they are viewed within the confines of particular states or seen in the perspective of the world as a whole. Physical mixing has produced new population varieties of significant size in places; *mestizos* in Latin America, Coloreds or Eurafricans in South Africa, Anglo-Indians or Eurasians in Asia. But the parent stocks from which they have sprung retain their identity so there is as yet still an increase rather than a decrease in the overall physical variety of mankind. And although some states are less diverse than others, populous Japan and thinly peopled Somalia having a high degree of ethnic homogeneity, even they possess distinctive minorities. Elsewhere the cultural and racial variety is substantial; in the great states of China, India, Russia and the United States of America where ethnic minorities or nationalities can number many millions, equivalent to whole nations elsewhere; in Brazil, Britain, Nigeria, Malaysia, Ethiopia, South Africa, each with its several peoples; or even in small states such as Fiji, Guyana, Mauritius, Trinidad and Tobago.

Despite the intensity of the western impact, to which reference was made at the beginning, it is significant and pleasing that peoples throughout the world have retained so much of their cultural as well as their physical individuality. This is certainly true of South-east Asia where J S Furnivall made his famous observations on the 'plural society'. In Burma and Java under British and Dutch rule he was compelled to acknowledge the reality of the western superstructure of power. But within both countries, as elsewhere in the tropics, he observed the persistence of a 'medley of peoples – European, Chinese, Indian and native', each retaining its own religion, culture and language, its own ideas and ways. In their political aspect the plural societies comprised 'separate racial sections', in the economic sphere there was a division of labor along racial lines. Furnivall's generalizations have been adapted and tested in the Caribbean, in Africa and in other parts of the world, and they have been criticized and sometimes rejected as inapplicable, but there can be no doubt that his perceptive observations have proved immensely stimulating to others seeking to understand the structure and processes of multi-racial and multi-cultural societies.

The significant and once widely used word 'native' in the above paragraph, following as it does a reference to European, Chinese and Indian, who have all achieved a world-wide distribution, rightly prompts a closer look at how local 'native' peoples have reacted to alien incursions. Some, sadly, have been overwhelmed and almost exterminated. Certain Australian Aboriginal and Amerindian tribes come readily to mind, as do the tiny Bush peoples of Africa. Yet others have been either more fortunate in their circumstances or more resilient. Although hard-used the Bantu-speaking African peoples of southern Africa have not only survived but have increased their numbers. Proud peoples like the Zulu, Swazi, Sotho and Tswana of South Africa, or the Ndebele and Shona of Rhodesia, have been subjected to dispossession from extensive areas of their ancestral lands, to labor practices which have disrupted family life, and to other harsh consequences of domination. But despite all their disabilities they have never reacted passively to conquest. Their corporate spirit endures.

Given an extreme case like South Africa it is easy to see how difficult it is to generalize accurately about vast human processes such as the 'western impact' or any other impact upon 'native' peoples. However, well-considered generalizations do provoke thought and they can be helpful, especially when they are made by scholars who in addition to their own reading have carried out detailed comparative field studies, and over substantial intervals of time. One such man, Sir Raymond Firth, has suggested that the meeting and mingling of western peoples with 'small-scale' Oceanic, East African and analogous communities tends to follow a cyclical pattern of four stages. At first meeting there is an exploration and acceptance of western ideas and materials by the native peoples which is followed by an attempt to absorb these into their traditional local system without a full appreciation of all the likely consequences. Thereafter, in the third stage, as the people come to be aware of difficulties, strains, and disappointments there is a reaction of disillusionment, even rejection. Finally, a wiser, and possibly a chastened, local people attempts a more realistic reintegration of western and traditional elements.

In his analysis of culture contact and social change Firth attached considerable weight to the effects of modern industrial technology. But even though its influences can be substantial, and although local communities might be forced to relate themselves to outside economic, political and religious structures, 'small-scale' peoples nevertheless tend to retain many of their local cultural elements. They keep to things like their types of food and styles of sleeping and greeting, and to the recognition of their group symbols and interests which give expression to their corporate distinctiveness. An important point is that what a local community normally seeks is not assimilation in the sense of complete incorporation but rather a more limited though real, and equal, honored participation in the larger and dominant system which encompasses them.

On the much debated subject of assimilation it is interesting to take note of the views of an individual 'native' leader of the caliber of Leopold Senghor, poet, philosopher, sometime-grammarian of the French constitution, president of Senegal. As an ideal for African and other peoples subjected to the assault of western cultural chauvinism he exhorts them to 'assimilate and not be assimilated'. Fellow Africans are thus urged to be active not passive in their responses to new or alien cultures and cultural elements. It is for them to take the initiative in selecting those aspects of western thought and practice which they believe will best fit in with their own valued ways and wishes. Senghor's life and experience has equipped him well to know the temptations and dangers of submitting to the insidious onslaughts of over-confident and powerful western nations. But he sees that to preserve self-respect, both for an individual or a whole people, it is necessary for African and negro peoples everywhere to take proper pride in their own distinctive and valuable institutions, their music, art and social systems. Only by knowing and appreciating what is their own, can they act from a position of strength in seeking to achieve desirable and rewarding syntheses with other cultures. Only through genuine mutual respect between peoples and cultures can there be hope of a durable and worthwhile universal civilization. Senghor has expressed these ideas attractively and forcefully but several other leaders and thinkers have contributed to this theme: Mahatma Gandhi, Pandit Nehru and Chief Albert Luthuli among them.

The west will do well to heed such ideas, for one of the most serious defects of imperialism was the blindness which afflicted its agents and prevented them from appreciating the merits of differing civilizations and cultures. Too frequently they were obsessed by notions of their own superiority. All peoples are ethnocentric to a greater or lesser degree but pride in large-scale scientific and technological success has afflicted all too many westerners. This very success should be seen to impose a special burden of responsibility on western peoples to be more sensitively aware of the rich though often fragile cultures from which they can learn so much of value to themselves. Sir Edward Evans-Pritchard has spoken of the tremendous personal debt which he feels he owes to the Nuer people in the heart of the Sudan, whose wisdom he has recorded so skilfully and appreciatively. But too many people in the west still firmly believe that in the process of inter-cultural exchange it is they who must do the giving rather than the receiving. The unreadiness to listen, coupled with ignorance of the reasons for age-old practices and unawareness of the delicate ecological balance between a people's culture and its physical environment have led to severe and avoidable damage harmful to mankind as a whole. The Xingu Indians of Brazil, the peoples of the Sahel suffering devastating drought in the southern borderlands of the Sahara, the Eskimo in the oil areas of North America, are but a few striking examples.

It is not difficult to itemize all the many areas of tension and conflict which have arisen between insurgent and local peoples in former colonial countries. Land, labor and political representation have provided some of the main issues. They continue to do so. But every aspect of human relationships can be important. Questions of access to public places, public transport, social clubs, sports facilities, have all given rise to strong inter-group feeling. Opportunities for school, college and university education, equality of social security and other benefits are obviously important also. Relations with police, adequate representation of all peoples in police and armed forces are other significant areas. Language, religious and other rights also raise problems which are best met by a generous and responsible approach on the part of all concerned. Numerous texts on ethnic and race relations deal more or less adequately with such topics, some attempting wide comparisons, others concentrating on single countries, some offering general theories or typologies, including lists of the major 'axes of relations' or the most significant types of race relations situations, others emphasizing rather the historical uniqueness of each national situation and dwelling on the virtual impossibility of adequate total comprehension of all the many and varied forces and factors at work.

It may be said, however, that most serious students are firmly at one in deploring the existence of 'color bars', or arbitrary racial discrimination, which represent the harmful manifestations of racial or cultural prejudice. This is true no matter whether the students are human biologists, that is scientists who are professionally expert in genetics, 'race biology' and the like, or social scientists working in psychology, social anthropology, politics or sociology. Much of real value to mankind still has to be discovered and applied by specialists in the human sciences but there is a heartening and overwhelming consensus among all of them that no people in the world of any race, color, historical or cultural condition need fear the outcome of further serious scientific research because there is no justification for racist policies nor any prospect that they will ever be deemed legitimate. Rather all peoples can be confident of the benefit which must result from sound scientific enquiry. In this connection it deserves to be said that virtually all the peoples of the world are racially mixed to some degree, and that the so-called mixed peoples, who now make up significant populations in every continent, are at least the equal of all other peoples in every respect, intellectual, moral, physical. Some would attribute an enviable hybrid vigor or special beauty to mixed peoples though most of them would simply ask to be regarded as neither superior nor inferior to others.

Thus far we have concentrated primarily on the relations between western and other peoples, an understandable emphasis we hope in the light of the history of recent centuries. But it is vitally important to the full understanding of the meeting, mingling and mixing of peoples that we widen our universe to include encounters and adjustments between Asian and African, Asian and Asian, African and African as well as other peoples, such as those of the Pacific. Before the age of western expansion there were great empires elsewhere and all kinds of relations between dominant and subject peoples, including enslavement and the imposition of alien beliefs and customs. Several such imperial advances and regional struggles were in fact halted by the western incursion. The Zulu empire and the Mogul empire are simply two instances which can be replicated in West Africa, Latin America and Indo-China. Powerful hierarchies had been established for many centuries in Ethiopia, the middle and near east, Mexico and China. Elaborate, strong and subtle systems of social stratification existed among the numerous peoples of India.

Once there was the definite prospect of western withdrawal, those old struggles for power which had been merely interrupted were resumed while fresh competition between new groupings was also initiated. Many students believe that much more effective action might have been taken by the western imperial powers to devise more suitable forms of government for those countries and peoples to whom power was suddenly transferred after so many years of empire. It is however a tragic fact that independence was very frequently marked by large-scale communal warfare, killing and destruction. The partition of India, the Nigerian Civil War, the Burundi and Rwanda massacres, the prolonged strife in Indonesia, provide cases of considerable ethnic conflict. More modest, though still serious, have been the struggles in successor states such as Guyana, where immigrant peoples of African and Indian origin have competed, and in Fiji where the Indian immigrants now outnumber the native Fijians. In both Guyana and Fiji there is urgent need for continuing attention to the systems of government and for continued wise leadership and agreement among all peoples in order to prevent disruption. Examples can be multiplied without difficulty; Malaysia and Sri Lanka (Ceylon), Vietnam, Sudan, Zaïre, Venezuela, Colombia, each has its own important minority questions and problems of sharing power and resources. As the giant Prime Minister of Fiji has observed, we do no service to mankind if we wear blinkers and avoid open discussion of ethnic and communal issues. It is infinitely better to face them frankly and constructively, confident in our ability to make sensible communal arrangements in the best interests of the society as a whole.

Besides the overseas regions of the world from which the west has withdrawn its imperial rule and where the western presence is now greatly reduced it is essential in any survey of the movements and meetings of the peoples of the world not to exclude the nations, nationalities or ethnic groups of metropolitan zones such as Europe and North America. This is particularly desirable now that simplistic notions of 'assimilation' have been abandoned in the face of evidence of how communities respond. Thus in the United States, where black Americans understandably oppose an imposed or compulsory segregation, it has been found that the ideal of the 'melting pot' has not been achieved. Italians, Irish, Jews, Poles, and numerous other elements have chosen to preserve their ethnic distinctiveness. Tangible benefits in employment, housing, education, marriage, have contributed to this result. Religious and cultural advantages have also been greatly valued. A similar response is to be seen in Canada among the immigrant nationalities of the mid-west quite apart from the deep-rooted recognition of French-Canadian language, religious and civil law rights, stemming from the Quebec Act of 1774.

That the peoples of Europe, the continent from which so many of the migrants to North and South America, to Australasia and southern Africa, originated, have preserved so much of their own individuality is also something which deserves attention. It is in fact enormously significant, yet all too frequently it is overlooked. There has been an excessive and dangerous preoccupation with 'color' and 'race' in its narrowest sense, with 'Whites' or 'Europeans' as against say 'Africans' and 'Asians'. It is this in part which explains the overlooking of the full significance of ethnic and cultural divisions in say Nigeria or Uganda, both of which were once catalogued as 'African states' in the run-up to independence in contrast with the 'multi-racial states' of Kenya and Northern Rhodesia. More perceptive and helpful policies might well have emerged if proper account had been taken in time of culture rather than race, and of books of the kind of *Welsh and Scottish Nationalism* by Sir Reginald Coupland published in 1954. In this study we were all reminded of the deep and fascinating history of conflict, compromise and co-operation between the English and the Welsh and Scots in Great Britain and of the relevance of this whole story to the wider Commonwealth and world. After several centuries the peoples of Great Britain choose to preserve their individuality. Unity not uniformity is still their preferred mode of living together. Greater awareness of the desire among peoples for cultural freedom and self-expression could well have helped when the substantial West Indian, Pakistani, Indian and African immigrations took place. All too much emphasis was placed on their being 'colored', a dubious blanket category, rather than say Barbadians, Jamaicans, Punjabis, Sierra Leoneans.

In Europe as in North America there has as yet been no 'melting pot'. The forces of industrialism, the compulsions of mass society, the effects of urbanization have not produced the predicted uniformity. On the contrary there has, if anything, tended to be a heightened clinging to distinctiveness. This might change in the Europe of the future, but meanwhile Walloons and Flemings within Belgium, Swiss of many kinds, and other nationalities, all contribute their own valuable qualities to the common pool. Mainland Europe like Britain has also had its own infusions of Asian and African peoples to add to the overall diversity.

There would be no point in trying to ignore the fact that conflict as well as co-operation has characterized the meeting and mingling of peoples. People today are still killed on the basis of primary ethnic identification in every continent. Problems of ethnic, cultural and racial adjustments also exist in every country. But it is wrong to see the meeting of peoples in a problem context alone. It is a natural perennial process from which enrichment and pleasure emerge and from which countless constructive advances in human history – philosophy, religion, art, science – have resulted.

Peoples of the Arab world

The term Arab describes a people who share the same language and the same cultural traditions. It does not refer to a distinct ethnic group or nationality or even religion. With the Arab conquest during the 7th and 8th centuries, the Arabic language reached a position of cultural dominance in Arabia and North Africa. Arab conquerors have influenced, and have been influenced by, the conquered peoples who were of different cultural, linguistic and social backgrounds. The majority of people in the Arab world and North Africa adhere to Islam; but there are other non-Arab groups such as Turks, Persians, Kurds, Circassians and Berber who also embrace Islam. Not all Arabs are Muslims. The contributions in this volume and the glossary do not claim to be an exhaustive survey of the peoples of the Arab world and North Africa. Covering an area of over five million square miles and inhabited by over 100 million people, the Arab world (commonly referred to as the Middle or Near East) and North Africa portray a variety of peoples, cultures, languages, religions, ecological conditions, political and economic organizations. The present volume shows some representative examples of the complexity of these two regions.

The Arab world and North Africa have witnessed the rise of numerous civilizations: Egyptian, Sumerian, Babylonian and Assyrian. The Arab world was successively a part of the Persian, Greek, Roman, Arab, Mongol, Tatar and Ottoman Empires. North Africa was part of the Carthaginian, Roman, Vandal, Byzantine and Arab Empires. During medieval times, European crusaders came and occupied the eastern shores of the Mediterranean in their attempt to free the Holy Land from the Muslims. Other more recent external influences such as the French, Spanish and Italians in North Africa, Syria and Lebanon, and the British in Jordan, parts of Arabia and Iraq, have also left their cultural and linguistic traits in these regions.

Despite the common linguistic and cultural heritage of the Arabs, there is diversity in their spoken language and in their ways of life. The classical Arab language is understood by educated Arabs in these regions, but there are many local dialects which sometimes cannot be easily understood between Arabs. The local dialects have been influenced by Persian, Turkish, French and English, in accordance with the foreign influence in a particular country. There are also people living within these regions whose mother tongue is not Arabic: the Kurds and Armenians, for example, speak languages which belong to the Indo-European stock.

The Arab world is the birthplace of three monotheistic religions: Judaism, Christianity and Islam. Islam appeared in Arabia during the 7th century and by the middle of the 8th century it had spread by conquest and conversion to North Africa and central Asia. Islam provides a religious way of life and a tradition for its adherents. The original teachings, however, have been diffused into a variety of traditions and practices. As with Christianity, there are a number of sectarian movements within Islam; the major two groups are the Sunnis and the Shi'ites, each of which is further divided. Within present-day Islam there are also a number of Sufi religious orders which are based on Orthodox Islam. Chief among these orders, which have come to play important political roles, are the Mahdiya in the Sudan and the Sanusiya in Libya.

In all the countries of the Arab world and North Africa, there are religious and national minorities. An example of this complexity is Syria where the following national and religious groups are to be found: the Arabs in Syria are either Muslim or Christian; the Arab Muslims are divided into various sects (Sunni, Shi'ites, 'Alawis and Ismailis). There are also two sects which are offshoots of Islam: Yezidis and Druzes. The Arab Christian community is composed of Greek Orthodox, Syrian Orthodox, Armenian Gregorians, Greek Catholics, Syrian Catholics, Chaldean Catholics, Armenian Catholics, Maronites, Nestorians and various Protestant sects. Lastly, the non-Arab groups in Syria are the Kurds, Turkomen and Circassians – all Sunni Muslims. Lebanon is another case where there are a number of Muslim and Christian sects, each with political importance. It is a country in which there is no single religious majority, Muslim or Christian. Here the government structure is maintained by a balanced distribution of government positions among various minorities.

The Jewish population in Israel portrays cultural, social, linguistic and religious diversity. The state of Israel was created in 1948 when many Palestinians were displaced. The growth in population of Israel has been characterized by large-scale immigration from different parts of the world within a very short period of time. Within Israel there are Jews who have emigrated from America, France, Russia and Britain, and from east European and Arab countries. The Jews speak Hebrew which, like Arabic, is a Semitic language; Hebrew also has variations in Israel, each of which differs in intonation, accent and loan words. The religion of the Jews is Judaism of which there are offshoots such as the Karaites and the Samaritans. There are strong economic, religious, cultural and emotional ties between Israel and Jewish communities throughout the world.

The Arab world occupies a strategic position: it links Europe, Africa and Asia. With the opening of the Suez Canal in 1869, a link of considerable commercial importance was established between the Mediterranean and the Red Sea. Because of this, and because of its oil resources, the Arab world and North Africa became a focus for the rivalries of the great powers. The area has suffered great political instability. There are differing régimes, ranging from monarchies to republics, military republics and emirates. Strong men seize power and are quickly overthrown. Parties are formed and banned and military takeovers are frequent. Another major cause of

In the last decade development has completely altered the face of Beirut, capital of Lebanon, as it has so many other cities in the Arab world.

(Center) Traditional patterns of life are being challenged by women as well as men as new wealth and industry bring education to everyone.

Greek Orthodox priests preach their view of Christianity beside the leaders of a vast number of other sects and religions.

The Middle East is the source of the three great monotheistic religions – Islam Judaism and Christianity. Most Arabs are Muslim.

this instability is the Arab-Israeli impasse and the problem of the Palestinian refugees.

Most of the countries of the Arab world and North Africa took their present political form between the two world wars. Nationalism has been a political force which has both united and divided the people of this area. Although the Arabs see themselves as one nation, the different régimes and political outlooks make aspirations towards unity difficult, if not impossible, to realize. In 1945 the Arab League was formed, which at the present time includes most countries of the Arab world and North Africa; it is a voluntary association aiming to strengthen the close ties linking these countries and to co-ordinate their policies and activities.

The problem concerning the rights of minorities has become prominent with the rise of nationalism. This area encompasses peoples of varying ethnic affiliation who have been intermixing for some time but it is by no means culturally homogeneous; separate minorities have preserved their identity.

A prominent feature of the Arab world and North

Only one man is entrusted with the key for the main gate of this Berber storehouse, although each family in the village owns a cell.

Africa is desert. The Sahara, Libyan and Arabian deserts occupy a considerable part of these regions. Much of the Sahara is rocky desert interspersed with areas of sandy desert with typical dune formations. There are two volcanic massifs: the Tibesti rising to 11,200 feet and the Ahaggar rising to 4,600 feet. The Arabian desert is a great plateau reaching a height of 2,000-3,000 feet fronted by mountains rising to 9,000 feet in Saudi Arabia and to an estimated 14,000 feet in Yemen; it is a huge and barren land relieved by occasional oases. Climatically the area comes within the Mediterranean zone which has long, hot summers and relatively mild rainy winters with short intermediate periods of autumn and spring. Three great rivers – the Nile, Tigris and Euphrates – are vital to almost half of the total population of the Arab world and North Africa who depend on these waters for agriculture. Their valleys are made up of rich and fertile alluvium, gradually deposited over many centuries, and they form the two ends of the fertile crescent which extends from the Nile valley through Israel, Jordan, Lebanon, Syria and Iraq.

The peoples who inhabit the plains and mountains of these regions have different modes of living and the articles in this volume demonstrate the variety of their social organizations. About 75 per cent of the people are settled agriculturalists, 15 per cent are urban dwellers and the remaining 10 per cent are nomads. Agriculture dominates the economies – providing between 20 per cent and 40 per cent of the national incomes of the countries of the Arab world and North Africa. Not all the arable land is cultivated and there is potential for improving agricultural output. One significant problem, the fragmentation of land holdings, continues to hinder agricultural development. Privately owned land is divided among heirs on the death of its owner in accordance with the Islamic laws of inheritance. Small plots of land are difficult to manage efficiently and fragmentation combined with simple agricultural methods results in a low yield and a low income. In a number of countries agrarian reforms, some of which have been successful, have been introduced. They have involved the redistribution of land holdings and a limitation on the size of plots. Wheat, barley and rice are the main subsistence crops whereas citrus fruits, dates and cotton are the chief cash crops which are exported to outside markets.

Despite the fact that the nomadic way of life is followed by a minority of people the nomad continues to be the popular stereotype of these regions. Most of the nomads are pastoralists whose livelihood depends on raising sheep and goats or breeding camels which they sell to settled peoples. Among the nomads the tribe, whose members are related through descent from a common ancestor, is an important political, economic and social unit. Each tribe has a sheik, a leader, whose position depends partly on descent and partly on personal merit. Some of the nomads in these regions constitute powerful political groups, such as the nomads in Jordan, Saudi Arabia and the United Arab Emirates. Nomads live in tents made of goat or camel hair and since they are mobile, they have few possessions. They follow a regular movement between desert oases and the fringes of cultivated areas and they visit villages and towns where they sell their products and livestock and where they obtain various goods. With the establishment of central governments the raiding and warfare between nomadic tribes has decreased. Attempts have been made to settle nomads (in Egypt and Saudi Arabia) and, with the discovery of oil, nomads are bypassing agricultural life. Attracted by the new wealth and opportunities of the oil industry they are moving directly from nomadic to urban communities.

Oil constitutes the main wealth of the Arab world and North Africa. It is to be found in Iraq, Kuwait, Bahrain, Qatar, the United Arabic Emirates, Oman, Saudi Arabia, Libya and Algeria, and in Egypt and Morocco which produce comparatively small quantities. North Africa is richer in other mineral resources than the rest of the Arab world – deposits of iron ore, lead, zinc and antimony are to be found and in Morocco there are extensive deposits of phosphate.

The majority of the peoples of these regions live in villages. Cities are growing rapidly with a variety of social life, political creed, contrasting wealth and poverty. The process of urbanization has accelerated enormously in the last few decades as a result of increases in population, improved communications, the effects of education and the development of oil resources which

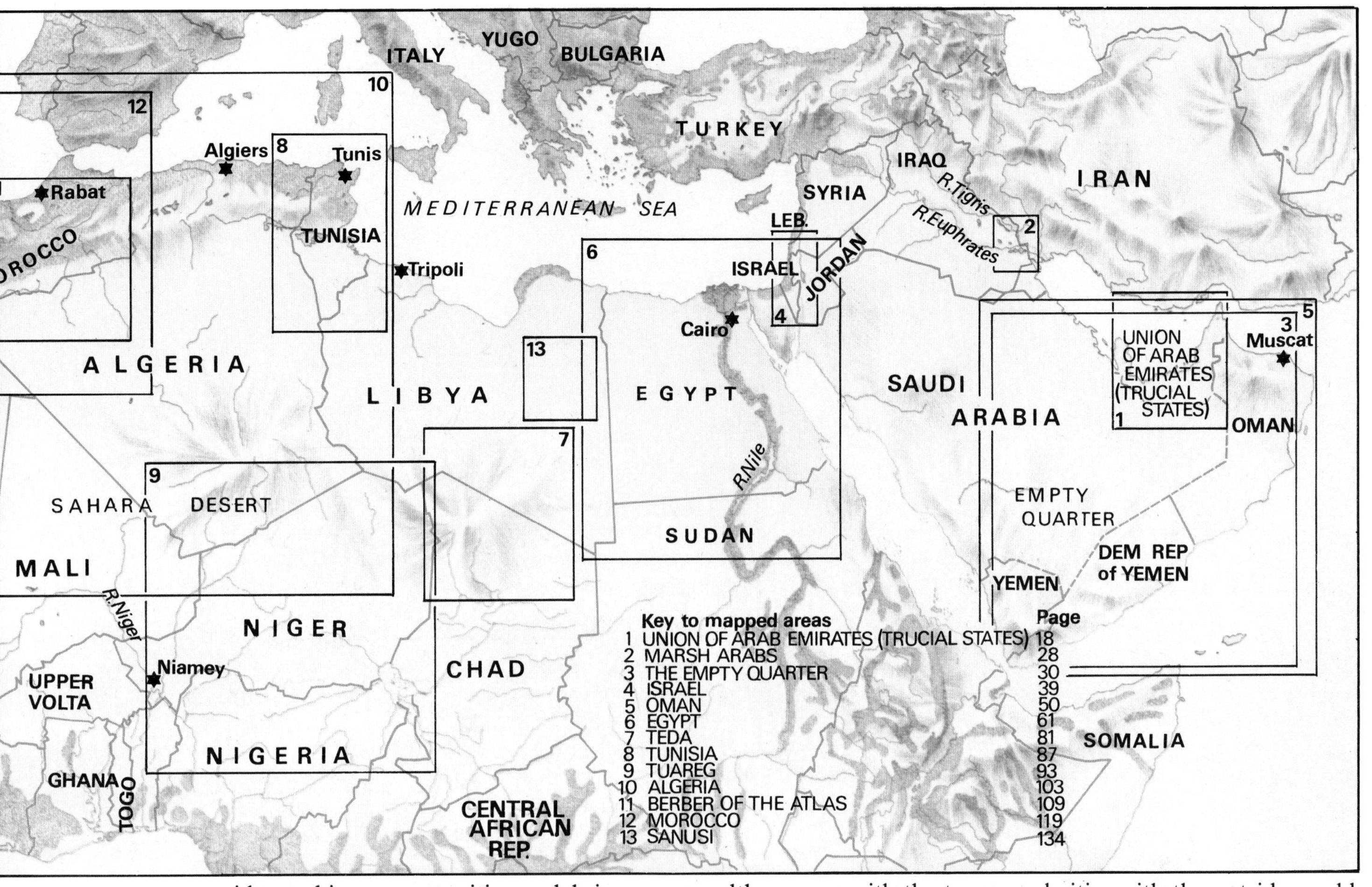

provide working opportunities and bring new wealth. Industrialization (on a major scale in Egypt and Israel and on a minor scale in Iraq, Lebanon and Syria) has drawn people from the countryside seeking employment. Traditionally, cities and large towns are divided into quarters or sections inhabited by religious, tribal, ethnic or occupational groups but these divisions are not so apparent nowadays. Shanty towns have developed around cities and problems of unemployment and lack of social services have arisen. Nearly all cities and large towns have modern suburbs which are growing rapidly in population mainly because of the influx of rural immigrants. Cairo has a population of 4 million, Alexandria and Baghdad between 1·5 and 2 million, Casablanca and Algiers about 1 million and Beirut, Damascus and Tunis about half a million.

Throughout the Arab world traditional religious, political, economic and social patterns are being challenged by the rising level of education, the impact of new and sudden wealth from oil and the effects of industrialization. Mass communications (radio, newspapers, television etc.) have widened the knowledge of both those living in cities and towns and of the peasants. Improved communications by road, rail and air have linked rural areas with the towns and cities with the outside world. There has been an improvement in standards of living, an emancipation of women, a decline in polygamy and a loosening of traditional kinship ties.

Communities reckon descent through the male line and the male head of the family has considerable authority. The extended family is still to be found in rural areas where it usually holds the land jointly. In cities and towns the elementary family is more common and here changes are more apparent: for instance, young people exercise personal choice in their marriage partners and in pursuing economic opportunities.

Aided by education and modern legislation, women are beginning to take their place in the economic and public life of their countries. Nevertheless, complex family ties and even tribalism still play a part in political, economic and social affairs. In the rapid changes confronting the peoples of the Arab world and North Africa there remain many problems. The chief of these are the search for a form of government able to bring stability to a constantly changing situation, and the reconciliation of growing secularization in some countries and classes with a return to the practices of traditional Islam in others.

Holy cities
The Arab world

Islamic holy cities possess a special sanctity for believers. They regard them as the places in which a full and truly Muslim life may be lived. These cities have acquired their holiness either by command of God or through a long-standing association with religious tradition. Believers make pilgrimages to them. Then Muslims from different parts of the world congregate in the holy cities where some of them have remained to form foreign communities. Religious schools, for the teaching of Islamic theology, have flourished in these cities. But tradition does not permit cinemas, theaters and other places of amusement. Apart from the religious significance of the pilgrimage, it provides a revenue through which the holy cities have gained a commercial importance. A central feature of every holy city is the shrine with a mosque attached to it. These have gilded or mosaic domes and minarets. Towns have grown up round these shrines and both have undergone periods of improvement and addition. The towns are no longer confined within their old walls which were built for protection; the increase in population, an influx of pilgrims and a rising wealth have resulted in a physical expansion and in the introduction of modern schooling, roads, hospitals, broadcast stations and other amenities.

There are two types of holy city. Cities like Mecca and Medina (in Saudi Arabia) and Jerusalem are visited by all Muslims. Other cities such as Najaf, Karbala, Kadhimain, Kufa and Samara (in Iraq), and Mashhad and Qum (in Iran) are revered and visited by the Shi'ites (an Islamic sect who consider that the prophet's cousin, Ali, should have been his successor).

For all Muslims the pilgrimage or *hajj* to Mecca and Medina is a religious duty; it is stated in the Koran that a Muslim must perform the pilgrimage once in his life providing that he is financially able to do so. During a pilgrimage, which takes place during the month of Dhu al-Hijja (the twelfth month of the Islamic year), a person must abstain from worldly affairs and must wear a special white garment. The pilgrimage consists of various rituals, the chief of which are standing before God on the plain of Arafat, stoning the devil, walking round the Ka'ba seven times, running seven times between the twin hills of Safa and Marwa, kissing the Black Stone and offering a sacrificial animal. Muslims who have performed the pilgrimage acquire the title of *hajj*.

Mecca, the foremost holy city of Islam, is significant for two reasons: it is the site of the Ka'ba and it is the birth-place of the prophet Mohammed and the scene of his earliest preaching. Mecca was a holy city before the coming of Islam, but the pilgrimage by Muslims to the House of God was started by the prophet, who made a pilgrimage to Mecca the year before his death. The Ka'ba, a sacred cube-shaped building near the center of the Great Mosque, is believed to have been built by Abraham and his son Ishmael at the command of God as a replica of God's house in heaven. In the Ka'ba lies the Black Stone, the chief object of veneration; it was originally the most venerated of the multitude of idols and sacred stones which stood in Mecca until the city was conquered by the prophet. The Great Mosque which surrounds the Ka'ba contains the famous well of Zamzam which is supposed to be the spring found in the wilderness by Hagar at the moment when her infant son Ishmael was dying of thirst. The water of this well is regarded by Muslims as a purifying agent and an infallible cure for diseases. Because of the holiness of Mecca, it has become the *qibla*, the direction to which all Muslims pray.

Medina is celebrated as the residence of the prophet after his emigration from Mecca and is his burial place. Medina was the capital of the Islamic Empire from the time of its occupation by the prophet in 624 AD until it was taken in 683 AD by the Umayyads, who transferred the capital to Damascus. It lost its political significance but it became a place of pilgrimage and the home of jurists and theologians. The pride of Medina is the Great Mosque, which was originally built by the prophet though additions and improvements were undertaken by successive rulers. The Mosque comprises imposing buildings with many doors and fine ceramic ornamentation. Built around a quadrangle, its open court is surrounded by colonnades. The chamber adjoining the Mosque contains the sacred tombs of the prophet Mohammed and the first three caliphs who succeeded him. It is supposed to contain also the tomb of Fatima, the prophet's daughter, the well of the prophet, and some palm trees said to have been planted by the prophet's daughter.

While Mecca was a sanctuary and a city of merchants before Islam, Medina was a city of agriculturalists and only became a place of pilgrimage after the death of Mohammed. Originally an oasis, Medina stands where swift-flowing streams converge. Dates and fruits are grown on the fertile volcanic soil and there is a modern date-processing factory. Besides agriculture, the people of Medina, who number nearly 60,000, derive an income from the pilgrims by renting them dwellings, acting as guides and from selling merchandise.

Jerusalem is not only a place of reverence for Jews and Christians but also for Muslims. The Dome of the Rock, known as Qubbat al-Sakhra, is revered by Muslims for it is from here that the prophet Mohammed is believed to have ascended to heaven on the occasion of his celestial journey. The rock forms the summit of Mount Moriah and here the Temple of Solomon was erected. Tradition relates that Abraham took Ishmael to sacrifice to God at the rock. Built originally in the 7th century AD, the present Dome is gilded with mosaic arabesque designs and is supported from the inside by marble pillars.

Shi'ite cities developed around shrines of much venerated imams. The imams are divinely appointed rulers and teachers of the faithful. The recognition of Ali, the prophet's son-in-law and cousin, as the legitimate successor of the prophet is the focal point of Shi'a

theology and represents a divergence from that of the Sunni, the other Islamic sect. The imams are believed to perform miracles and act as mediators between God and the believers. There are twelve imams; the last one, Al-Mahdi, is supposed to have vanished but it is believed that he will reappear to establish the true faith on earth.

Pilgrimages to the shrines of imams are made during the month of Muharram, the first month of the Islamic year. Shi'ites from Iraq, Iran, Afghanistan, India, Pakistan and other places come to visit these shrines. A visit indicates devotion and duty and is a means of acquiring merit and blessing. The most binding oaths are taken at the tombs of imams and at their shrines pilgrims purchase prayer beads, shrouds and tablets of sacred earth. The longing of every Shi'ite to find a last resting place in the shadow of one of the imams, particularly Ali, has meant that extensive cemeteries have been laid out at the great Shi'ite centers of pilgrimage as well as at Mecca and Medina.

Najaf is revered because it contains the tomb of Ali, the founder of the Shi'a sect. It is believed that Harun Al-Rashid built a shrine around the tomb in the 8th century AD. Another town connected with Ali and visited by the Shi'ites is Kufa which is the site of his death. Other Shi'ite holy cities grew up around the tombs of imams who are Ali's descendants. Karbala contains the shrines of Al-Husain, a son of Ali, and of his half-brother, Al-Abbas. It is also the site of the battle of Karbala (680 AD) in which Al-Husain and Al-Abbas were killed. Pilgrimages to Karbala are believed to have begun as early as the 7th century AD. While Kadhimain contains the tombs of the seventh and ninth imams, Samara contains the tombs of the tenth and eleventh. Samara is also revered because there the last imam, Al-Mahdi, disappeared in the 9th century AD. In Iran, where most of the people are Shi'ites, there are a number of holy cities, chief of which are Mashhad and Qum. Mashad contains the tomb of the eighth imam; the shrine area is a large complex of religious buildings including the beautiful turquoise domed mosque of Gowarshad, built by the wife of Shah Rokh in 1414, and the golden dome of the shrine itself, built in the 15th century and redecorated by Shah Abbas in 1606. Mashhad is the only Shi'ite holy city in which modern industries and cinemas have been introduced. Qum contains a number of shrines including that of Fatima, the sister of the eighth imam.

(Top) Pilgrims walk seven times around the Ka'ba at Mecca, birth-place of the prophet Mohammed and the holiest of all Islamic cities.

Pilgrimage to Mecca and Medina, *hajj*, is a religious duty which the Koran commands every Muslim to do once in a lifetime if he can afford it.

People of the Trucial Coast

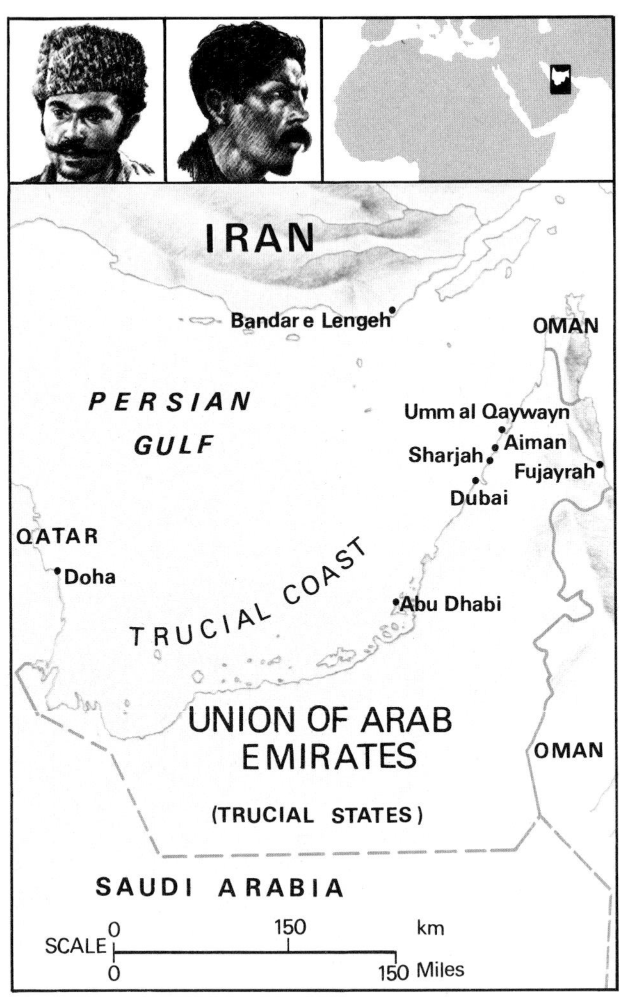

The Trucial States – now the Union of Arab Emirates – occupy a geographical area that one can call west Oman, projecting northwards as a horn of the Arabian peninsula. About 200,000 people, of whom approximately half are recent immigrants, are unevenly distributed over the 30,000 square mile triangle of land. Most is desert but, towards the north and east, a sparse scrub adds its grazing value to transient seasonal growths of grass. A back-bone of mountains runs along the eastern side of the triangle, between two narrow bands of plain watered by the mountains' outflow below ground and, sporadically, above it. To the south it merges with the bleak expanses of the Rub al Khali or Empty Quarter, a vast and barren area of sand occupying the whole interior of south Arabia. Where it merges Buraymi, a thickly peopled district, lies on a site that has long been a cross-roads for trade between the interior of Arabia and the rich ports and agricultural districts of the eastern seaboard. It was always the region's principal hinterland settlement, though it remained essentially a tribal one belonging to the interior. Now it has become the secon-

A silent, reverential banquet for the Sheik of Abu Dhabi. Vastly rich in oil, Abu Dhabi existed until the 1950s on a few date palms and frankincense.

In the seemingly casual, whispered meetings of the *Majlis*, the Sheik and his dignitaries conduct the affairs of state without formality.

(Bottom) The most crucial factor in the tribespeople's support for their Sheik lies in the tradition of free access to his counsel.

dary capital of Abu Dhabi, territorially the largest of the seven Trucial States.

The almost weird stimulation of oil wealth produces modernities in the society of the Trucial States alongside the things of the traditional Arabian way of life which continue to persist. Variations range between the urban sophisticate and the rustic, between the modern and the traditional, and between the cosmopolitan in the coastal cities and the tribesman of the interior. But all these societies can be understood in terms of three social and cultural elements.

One of these elements is represented by the Shihu and Habus people living mainly in the high valleys and plateaux of the mountain chain. These highlanders' societies are strikingly unlike the coastal towns' societies and those of the lowland peoples of the interior. Lacking settlements of any size in their northern fastnesses these mountaineers retain a wild rusticity and remain ruggedly insular in their dealings with others around them. Artistically vigorous, they stand out as singers and dancers, weavers of brilliantly colored saddlebags and makers of distinctive pottery.

The second element comes from outside Arabia altogether. Intrusions from the sea represent an ancient, almost permanent feature of social life and history throughout the peninsula's eastern side. All communication with west Oman has been by sea because of the insecurity inherent in the tribal conditions of the interior, together with the sheer size and relentless aridity of the Rub al Khali which isolates the region from all the rest of Arabia except east Oman. Apart from a rare caravan along the coast from the west, and an occasional expeditionary force from emirates in central Arabia, almost nothing has come overland to Oman. Despite the inability of any power to maintain security at sea before the 19th century and despite west Oman's early reputation for bleakness, ferocity and want, there was a steady movement of people into the region from the sea. Enterprising individuals were deposited wherever social conditions allowed trade routes to spring up, adding non-tribal sectors to the populations, building up and urbanizing coastal centers that had developed in the tribal milieu during the 18th century with people from Iran, Iraq and the Indian sub-continent. This polyglot population supplied labor and was prominent in trade. It became socially integrated with other groups while remaining politically subordinate to the tribal factions and supra-tribal leaderships derived from the social environment of the interior.

The third principal element in the social constitution of west Oman comes from tribal Arabia. A world empire and a world culture was born in the Arabian interior in the 7th century: Islam. Thereafter, until the discovery of oil, it remained an uncoveted backwater of the world The more-or-less-tribal societies of the main body of Arabia are, beneath the regional variations,

The complex tangle of pipes and gauges must seem like some strange and exotic many-armed goddess of wealth to the people of Dubai.

(Over page) Enormous kohl-rimmed eyes peer alluringly over a camel leather mask. Oil wealth has begun to free women from their seclusion.

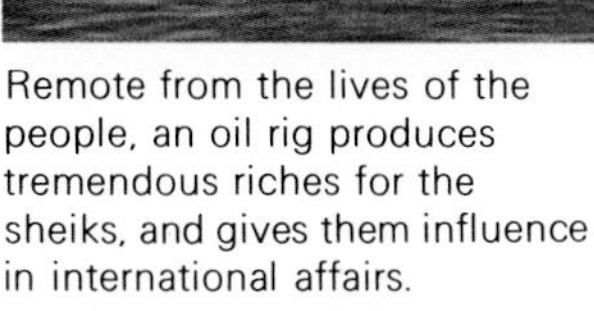

Remote from the lives of the people, an oil rig produces tremendous riches for the sheiks, and gives them influence in international affairs.

In the 19th century, Dubai creek grew from little-used fishing waters to the main entrepôt port of the eastern end of the Persian Gulf.

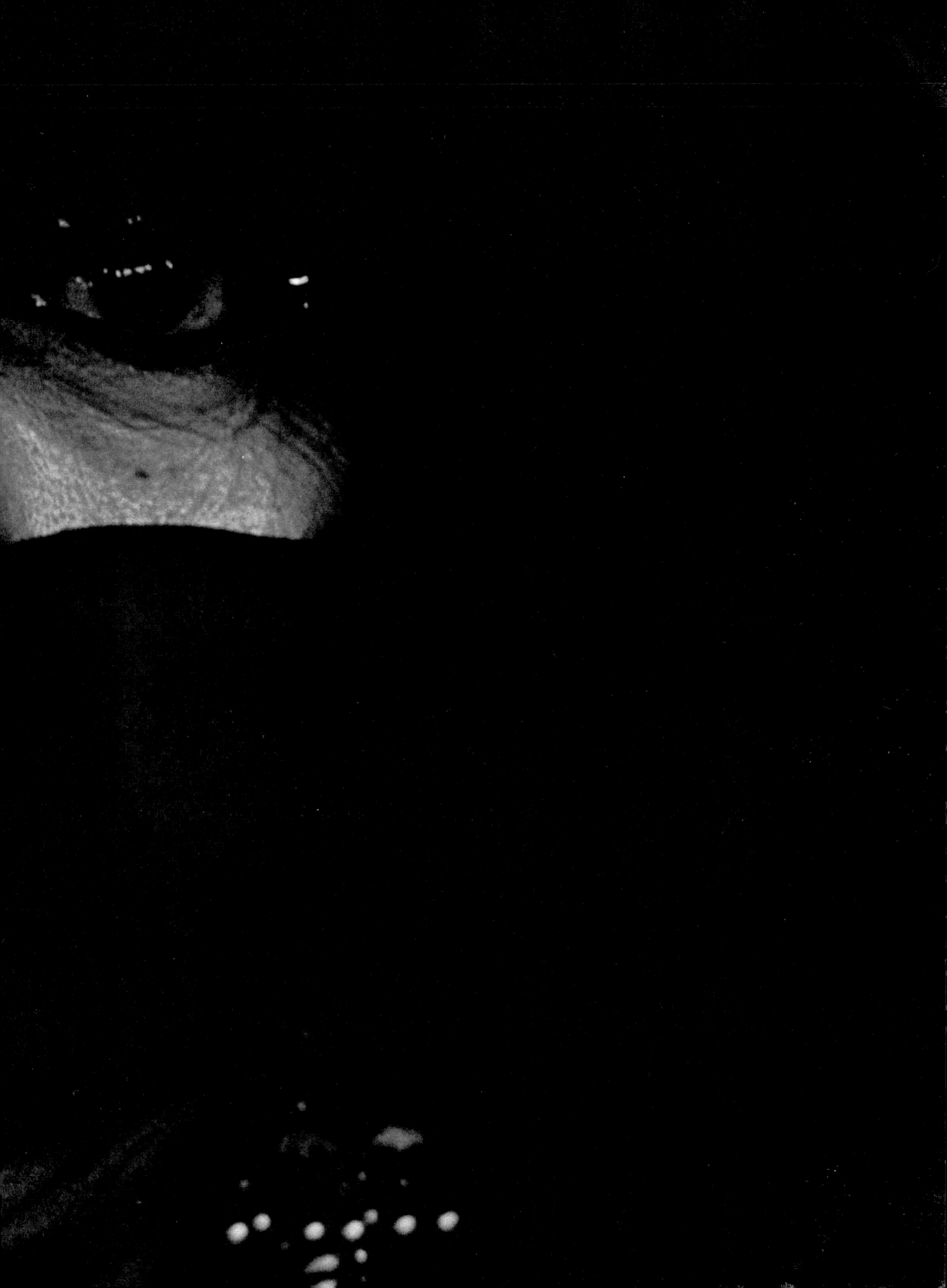

(Bottom) Harem women in Dubai paint their hands with henna in preparation for wedding celebrations. This special design is of an apple.

Even the feet of rich Arab women are embellished. The soles are brushed with henna, the toenails with enamel and rings decorate the toes.

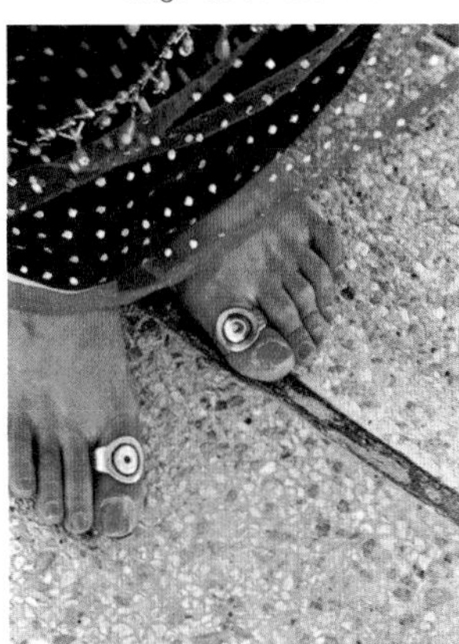

Gold jewelry, bracelets and earrings show the status of a woman – the richer her jewels the more important she is. Only crescents are worn by all.

(Right) A Sheika with a cigarette reveals her people's remarkable taste for combining the traditional with the modern and sophisticated.

substantially similar and consistent, making up a single medium of stark and simple forms. The medium is characterized by a balance uniting desert and oasis in a single world of agriculturalists, nomadic pastoralists – who alone can use the desert – and people whose existence falls between these extremes, combining elements of both. This balance is one of polar contrasts in human experience, as in scenery. The nomad wakes to endure the sun: the oasis agriculturalist wakes to toil in his plantation's shade. The nomad's environment is one of inescapable heat, glare, and shortage – of the attrition, total exposure and physical emptiness of desert existence – alleviated by space, movement and the freedom from disease inherent in shadeless aridity continually sterilized by the sun. The agriculturalist is generally better fed, wealthier and better sheltered; but he lives as though confined in the dirty and malarial conditions of the oasis. To the two of them, even the simplest experiences have opposite connotations. To the oasis dweller, immobility means release, ease, sociability and relaxation in the shade after the day's labors; for nomads, the epitome of immobility is that of the summer camps when large numbers of people are pinned down for months in crowded, dirty and miserable conditions to the few wells that outlast the drought.

A Beduin woman in Abu Dhabi perfumes her clothes with incense. In the desert where water is scarce, perfume may replace it as a freshener.

The import and export of gold and silver has compensated for the decline of the pearl trade and plays a part in the lives of many townspeople.

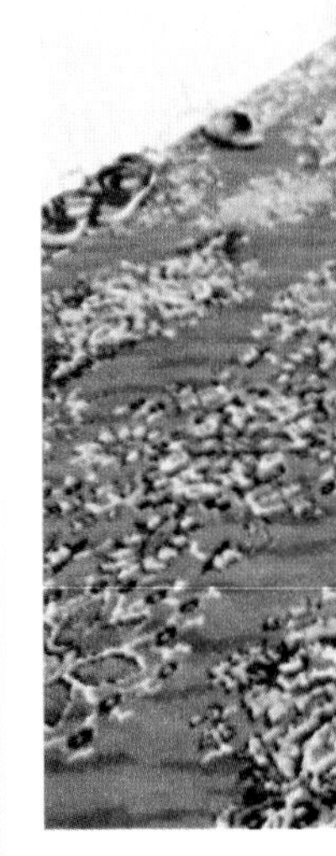

(Bottom) With a gold encrusted gun, a Dubai tribesman dances during the three weeks' celebration of the marriage of the Crown Prince to Sheika Alia.

Arabian nomads are Beduin. They are animal herding tribesmen who depend on the camel for transport and for much of their food. They live in goat-hair tents and move their entire household in pursuit of grazing for their animals every few days throughout much of the year. They live largely on their animals' milk products and to a lesser extent on their meat, on dates and on small amounts of rice or unleavened bread. They are not so much animal farmers as the hunters of scattered and ephemeral pastures which emerge in response to dews or local rainfalls. Where the ground is unproductive and waterless, they must move often and far. Where it is well watered life is easier and more flexible.

Since tribal conditions have been subordinated to state authority, radical changes have come to the hinterland. Freed from tribal raids, the agriculturalist has a viable occupation and an expanding market for the surpluses he can produce. But the Beduin has lost his lucrative role as an uncontrollable political force. His function as a provider of transport and safe passage along trade routes through his territory has disappeared. His camels have lost their significant market value and retained only a domestic value. A few enterprising nomads have moved into other activities, cultivating date gardens with modern machinery, repairing broken-down transport on the lonely desert tracks, hiring out their services as drivers and, in one or two cases, setting up small shops in the countryside. But most are simply losing their interest in camels. Their inherited independence makes it extraordinarily difficult for them to fit into modern industry.

Most of the population, if one includes the enormous influx of immigrants, now lives in the towns. After the struggle in which the coastal emirates extended their influence over the hinterland it is widely thought that the political significance of the hinterland has waned. But the towns' past is still rooted in the tribal background.

The history of Abu Dhabi shows how the emirates grew to importance. At some time in the 18th century drinkable water was found at Abu Dhabi – on the coast of a stretch of desert belonging to the Beni Yas – a powerful Beduin tribe. As camel breeders they had no interest in this barren coastline. Towards the end of the 18th century certain Beni Yas tribesmen had reached a state of destitution, having suffered the nomads' major misfortune of being raided out of Beduin existence. They settled as fishermen around the newly discovered water supply on Abu Dhabi island, and the colony thrived so well that the tribal sheik moved his own base there at the turn of the century.

A decline in world demand for natural pearls, and the massive production of cultured ones elsewhere, gave the emerging states a severe economic reverse in the first half of the 20th century. The pearling industry collapsed. A sad, rather beautiful heap of oyster shells still lay in Dubai's new banking district in 1969. But the basis of

Whole families and their friends come for the wedding celebrations. Many women stay in the harems and are segregated from the men at mealtimes.

the capital's existence was sound and not essentially economic. Dealing in precious metals lucratively replaced dealing in pearls. Shortly after the middle of the century, the discovery and exploitation of oil began to give additional economic support to the emerging states.

Arabian environments have shown before now that they can absorb radical and sudden change. The explosive appearance of the oil industry upon a scene already undergoing swift and radical change does, however, intensify certain inherent dangers. The chief danger is the politically dangerous likelihood that these countries will not develop as integral national societies at all, but as deeply divided populations afflicted with a 'state machine' of hastily assembled, alien infrastructure and 'welfare'.

As yet, however, change wears a glad and positive air. Increasing prosperity is improving the material conditions of life and health. Even deep in the hinterland tribesmen dress better and live more safely and satisfactorily than their grandfathers did. A flowering of arts and crafts and a sudden sophistication of clothing and jewelry, both traditional and modern, shine strongly against the austerity of traditional Arabia: and advances in education, law and administration accompany those which strike the eye more immediately. But the character of life remains Arabian. Indeed the future for these States depends heavily upon the extent to which it can do so, mediating modern processes with institutional forms that belong to west Oman.

The servant women of the harems attend the celebrations without surveillance – but they are still masked and clothed from head to foot.

Marsh Arabs
Iraq

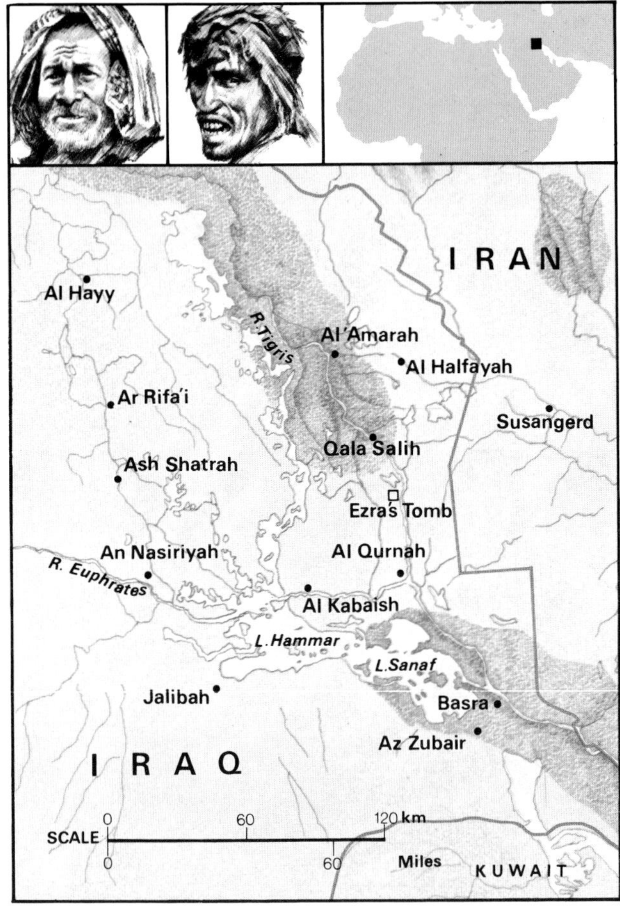

Throughout the middle east, land is plentiful and water is in short supply – except in the great marshes of southern Iraq where conditions are exactly the opposite. Here, the waters of the Tigris and Euphrates rivers overflow and spread over 6,000 square miles before gathering in the Shatt al-Arab and emptying into the Persian Gulf. Since before the times of recorded history, men and women have lived in these marshes, built houses on mounds of reeds, developing a technology as specialized as that of their neighbors, the desert nomads.

In the 1950s the population of the marshes of southern Iraq was estimated at 400,000. Open lakes, channels, islands, permanent marsh lands, seasonal and temporary marshes – in all these places, men were able to make a living: lakes and channels for fishing and transportation, islands providing land where reed-framed houses may be built and where crops may be planted. Temporary marshes vary in extent according to yearly flood levels and may revert to either grazing land or arid desert as water levels fall. The seasonal and permanent marshes offer the best environment for people, for here land can be diked, drained and cultivated, or left to the natural growth of the *qasab* or reeds which are essential to the marsh economy. But in past centuries these people developed two patterns of subsistence, and more recently a third has been added.

The great majority of marsh dwellers make their living by a combination of agriculture and raising cattle and sheep. Summer crops of rice and millet alternate with winter crops of wheat and barley, a pattern found elsewhere in southern Iraq. Vegetables are cultivated for sale in the nearest village and towns. Particularly in the north-western regions of the marshes, cattle products are also sold – milk, cheese, butter and cattle-dung are taken daily to nearby market centers, usually by the women. Holy men (*is-sada*), regarded as sons of the Messenger of God because of their claim to descent from the Prophet Mohammed, live among these settled marsh cultivators and are accorded special respect. In exchange for their services in lending religious sanctification and merit to tribal activities, the *sada* are supported by the tribespeople.

The tribal cultivators of the Iraqi marshes, like the Beni Isad of the southern region, proudly trace their descent from Arabian tribes and look down on the buffalo breeders, or Ma'dan, whom they regard as inferior in birth and occupation. Until recently this has reserved for the Ma'dan a monopoly over buffalo breeding and a unique position as aquatic nomads in the marshes. Water buffalo breeding, the second traditional subsistence activity, is largely confined to the permanent marshes. The reeds which grow there in abundance are the major source of food for these buffalo. But the Ma'dan, depending exclusively on buffalo herds, make up only a quarter of the total population of the marshes.

The Ma'dan generally live in scattered settlements, frequently making their homes on man-made islands of reed matting, which rise and fall with the floods. Family-owned herds range in size from one to ten animals and these must be constantly moved about in the marshes to graze on young green reeds or on the stubble of harvested fields. Both men and women herd and milk the buffalo, unlike the tribal cultivators among whom milking cattle is considered women's work. The Ma'dan are tribally organized and bound to share in the compensation payments levied against their tribal division for killing or injuring others. They are Shi'ites and tribal membership is based on patrilineal descent groups.

A third major occupation for marsh dwellers has developed in recent years. As the country-wide demand for reed mats increased, thousands of tribesmen began to weave mats not only for their personal use but also for the commercial market. These large mats of split woven reeds, a basic part of all buildings in the marshes, are used throughout southern Iraq for floor covers, roofs, temporary shelters and many other purposes.

As among other tribes of southern Iraq, the sheik traditionally collects tribute from the tribesmen to maintain the *mudhif*, the tribal guesthouse, which is the center of the political and judicial life of the tribe.

Together with respected tribal elders, the sheik resolves disputes among the tribesmen and carries out diplomatic negotiations with other tribes. The tribal *mudhif* is a gathering point for religious celebrations and daily prayers, and also the place in which hospitality is offered to strangers and tribesmen alike. Here, too, an elaborate and formal etiquette for greeting and seating among tribesmen demonstrates the differences in status of both groups and individuals.

Superficially, many of these people seem like Beduin who have simply transplanted the social and cultural ways of the desert and plains to a different environment. However, the marsh dwellers have developed their own social system, which is ordered according to the occupations and divisions of labor special to the marshes.

Until the 20th century, the marshes remained largely independent of outside political control. This was because of the unmapped and largely unexplored areas of the marshes, the difficulties of transport and communication, and also because of the dangers from wild boar and sudden storms. Yet the marshes have always been open to immigration from surrounding areas. Thus a people, whose ancestors may date from Sumerian and even more ancient times, has been supplemented over the centuries by individuals and groups driven into the marshes through defeat at the hands of their enemies, or after escaping from slavery and serfdom.

Ordinary tribesmen are traditionally accorded differing degrees of respect according to their age and conformity to tribal standards of good conduct. Cultivation was regarded as the only appropriate way of life for a respectable tribesman, until World War I brought a great increase in the demand for reed mats; mat-weaving for the commercial market has now been reluctantly accepted as an alternative and more secure source of income. This, however, has yet to be considered as respectable as the traditional occupations of the past.

For centuries, the marshes have provided their people with almost all the necessities of daily life, as well as ample means to trade for what they lacked – salt, tea, sugar, cloth and guns. Widespread drainage of the marshes will open a new and important agricultural resource for southern Iraq. And the enduring ecological balance reflected in the traditional ways of life will be replaced by a new range of human control over the marshes.

(Top) A *tarada* carries a load of reeds for the mat weavers. Its high pointed prow makes passage easier through the dense growth of reeds.

Lavosh, flat round bread, baked against the side of a mud oven heated with charcoal, has been made this way since biblical times.

An old man in his reed house. Until this century the marshes remained isolated and inaccessible, an ideal refuge for escaping slaves or serfs.

Empty Quarter
Saudi Arabia

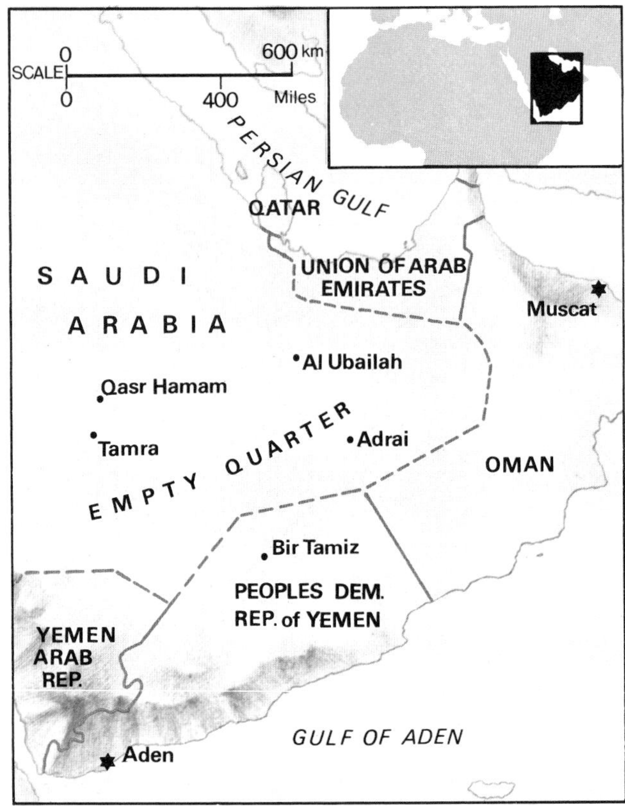

The deserts of the Arabian peninsula extend over more than 2.5 million kilometers. The south-eastern part of them, the so-called Rub al Khali – the Empty Quarter – covers about half of that total. It is in fact desert within the desert and it is so immense and desolate that the scattered tribes living in its border zone since times immemorial used to speak of the Empty Quarter as al Bahr as-Safi – the Pure Sea – meaning the Sea of Sand.

This part of the Arabian peninsula was the last explored part of our earth. Why was this? The place was empty. The Bedouin story-tellers spoke of the Beni Ad, the unbelievers, who, many centuries ago, had lived in an Arabia with more water and more vegetation. They were builders of stone monuments, simple structures of stone slabs and pieces of rock, and they had scratched pictures of camels, men, arrows and so on on the shiny brown layer of encrusted sand covering the boulders that fell from the wadi walls. And it was said these Beni Ad had built a town somewhere deep in the heart of the Sea of Sand. But these stories did not impress the western archaeologists. The other reason for staying away from this part of Arabia was its lack of security. The tribes living in the border zone were unruly, practically independent tribes, making war on each other and not obeying any of the Arab governments bordering the Empty Quarter.

The first explorer from the west was a German, Alfred von Wrede. He pretended to be a Muslim from Egypt, and in 1843, approached the Empty Quarter from the south. Half a century later, in 1892 another German, Leo Hirsch and a British couple, the Bents, made explorations in southern Arabia, but did not penetrate the Empty Quarter. The men who shouldered that task and put aside the veil of mystery hiding the Empty Quarter were three Englishmen: Bertram Thomas, Harry St John Bridger Philby and Wilfred Thesiger. After them were no more undiscovered secrets. They were the last to explore in the classical way, that is from the back of a camel or plodding on foot behind their caravans, the most tiring but the best way of gathering information and material. This was the way von Wissmann and I traveled on our expeditions in the southern borderlands of the Empty Quarter.

In May 1931 von Wissmann and I reached the most easterly part of the British Aden Protectorate. It was a protectorate in name only and in reality it was a completely independent territory. This Hadhramaut valley was the homeland of 99 per cent of the Arab emigrants to the Dutch East Indies. That is why my government ordered me to try and reveal this nearly unexplored part of Arabia and to report on its political and social conditions. I asked my friend von Wissmann to accompany me and to do the route-mapping and various other scientific work.

Finally we stood at the border of the Empty Quarter. We did not want to go on into a land of total emptiness after what we had witnessed in that island of prosperity, the homeland of the rich Arabs from the Dutch East Indies. We had seen where and how it ended and we turned our backs upon that uninviting scorched land where vegetation and animal life seemed to end. We wished 'God speed' to the rare, small and practically unladen caravan that crossed our path. But when we stopped for the usual exchange of news we received an absolutely unexpected reply: 'They say that a foreigner, a *nasrani* (Christian) accompanied by some daring Dhufari tribesmen, is trying to cross the empty sands, traveling north-east towards Qatar.' We stared at them in amazement. How did they, how could they know? Hundreds of miles of practically empty country were between us and that lonely white man – Bertram Thomas – and his small company. What a mysterious instrument is the desert telegraph!

Philby set off a few weeks later into the Empty Quarter. He documented important geographical data on this area. But there was still important work to be done and that was the task of Wilfred Thesiger. Thesiger was physically strong enough and believed in the task just as much as his desert-companions put their trust in Allah's guidance. And so they dared, together, to try what no westerner nor Arab had done before them nor was to do after them. They crossed and re-crossed the Empty Quarter and traveled extensively through its borderlands. They knew

A Muslim always carries his prayer rug so that wherever he is he may fulfil the prophet's command to pray three times each day facing Mecca.

The camel provides the Beduin with transport, meat and milk. It is worth about $100 and its meat, when cooked, tastes like veal.

where and when to trek, following the blessing of the rain, knowing that here and there the desert would produce sparse vegetation, enough to keep their animals alive.

Thesiger was a master of the human contact and that was the secret of his success in overcoming the fantastic hardships and discovering the mysteries of the Empty Quarter. His predecessors were not less important, for they had drawn the world's attention towards this long forgotten and unknown part of the earth. They did most of the technical side of the discovery. They showed Thesiger the way and so inspired him to the task he had to round off.

The tribes living in the borderlands of the Empty Quarter are few and only a few tribesmen travel inside it after the season's rains. They do not risk going too far away from their base-wells so that they can fall back on a sure supply of water. What it was like to live so very close to the edge of survival von Wissmann and I tried to find out when in May 1939 we traveled into the country where the Awamir tribe lived. Starting from the Wadi Hadramaut we had been walking with our guide, a few camels and their men. We searched in vain for human beings, as we approached the places where the Awamir were said to live with their flocks. We saw a gazelle, fleeing in the distance. Later on we met a caravan of four camels and with it two men, an old woman and two small children. Then we passed two square mud built houses or fortresses. In the distance we spotted more of these square towers, excellent landmarks in this featureless land. It looked as if we were approaching the inhabited Awamir world. On the rock-plateau we came across two small dykes, several miles long, which had been built to catch rainwater and to lead it towards the wide wadi with low sides on whose western border the square towers were standing. The Beduin here lived partly in primitive houses and partly in grottos under overhanging rocks. The grottos were closed off by walls of stones loosely piled on top of each other. The houses stood together above the wadi on the rocky slope. Primitive and clumsy square towers protected the houses that huddled around them. The lower walls were made of piled-up stones and the upper parts of mud. The houses were of piled stones and some of them were covered with branches supporting a loam roof. Man and beast lived together in these houses and grottos.

This Awamir settlement still had the stamp of war and plunder on it. The soil and its water supply did not provide adequate means of existence so the inhabitants tried to improve their standard of living by robbery.

Agriculture was neglected in favor of raising cattle because herds could be moved away and hidden. These weak tribes suffered bitterly at the hands of plundering neighbors and had nearly died out. Thus the dry lands became ever poorer and emptier. The bombs from British planes that burst over the central settlement of the strong neighboring tribe of the Sei'ar must have sounded like a message of hope to the much weaker Awamir. Peace has now spread over these wadis. None of the men we saw carried a rifle. These weapons had suddenly lost relevance and dropped in price now that the British Government had changed its so-called protection into reality.

Near this settlement there was water. A high dam had been built closing off an inward bend in the wadi wall, cleverly making a deep reservoir. Rain water drained into it and was stored there. The Awamir called these water reservoirs *kharif*. If the one here contained water, there was, we argued, good hope of others in the area. Four Beduin girls were busy watering their sheep and goats. The animals were small, perhaps because of the scarcity of fodder. Camels are not allowed to drink the best water: their water was a little farther ahead. There we had to fill the water-bags, then pour the water from the bags into our aluminium cooking pots out of which the camels drank one after the other. The quantity they stowed away was amazing.

A little boy who had joined our caravan in the afternoon said goodbye, taking two camel calves with him. He set off into the invisible, far distance, where his people were living. His mother would be there. With a happy smile on his brave little face he took leave of us and counted on being home by nightfall. He led the two young camels on a cord. He had no food or water, both he could find at his home grotto but on the way there he would have to do without. He set off into the vast emptiness. This was his world and he was convinced that it was a good and beautiful one.

After days of walking behind our small caravan we were now near our goal: Bir Tamiz. In the wadi walls were many grotto dwellings, abandoned by the Beduin. The people were now in the plains with their flocks. Later in the year they would return to seek protection from the cool nights in the oblong, shallow caves that they had closed off from the wadi with loosely piled stone walls. Then, unexpectedly, we came to a place where men must have recently been and in great numbers. It was the last resting place of those wandering through the borders of the Empty Quarter whose earthly journey had come to an end. The companions of their long wanderings seem to have wished to leave them well cared for. On a flat stretch of the bank, still in the wadi, but at a safe height above the flood-level, the great Awamir cemetery lies. It was close to the junction of the Wadi Jari and the Wadi Mahredun. A huge piece of rock that had fallen down from the wadi wall was its center and close to that rock lay the biggest and most carefully composed tombs.

Each of these tombs had two slabs of stone set upright, one at the head and one at the foot, in accordance with Islamic practice all over the world. Further from the rock were oblong piles of stones, the tombs of the poor, which must have numbered more than a hundred. The perpendicular form of the rock was full of holes and had been used as a depository for offerings. Into these cavities that nature had formed in the porous limestone rock wooden pegs had been driven. The barrels of old rifles had been hammered into the rock. We saw round eating mats, bags woven from the leaves of the dwarf palm and dried skins that had been used as water bags. A bottle swayed to and fro in the breeze. Fragments of camel saddles and even some empty kerosene tins in plaited baskets had found their way here. We counted at least ten rifles, until recently the most costly and valued possession of the Beduin. A Beduin cradle stood leaning against a smaller rock. It was the practical type that the Beduin mother takes with her everywhere, pressed closely to her hip. Some sad mother must have left this cradle of her little one near its grave. Her spell of maternal happiness had been short; the hard, never-

Sulaiyil is one of the oases on the edge of the Empty Quarter: a welcome sight to weary desert travelers.

(Top) Hamid, a desert guide, uses the sun as a compass. In three minutes he can fix the party's position to within a mile.

ending wandering with the flocks had to start again and there was no point in carrying an object that had become superfluous. Our companions said that this was a place where *walis* (saintly people) lay buried and that the Beduin who starts on a long journey leaves his weapons and those houshold articles he can spare in such a place for later collection, convinced that nobody will dare to intrude and steal them.

After a short trek further to the north we arrived at the Bir Tamiz. To our great astonishment it was not a well, but a reservoir. Under a thin layer of sand in the wadi lies massive rock. Bir Tamiz was a hole in this rocky bottom, a cistern made by the hand of nature, not of man. Allah was its creator. The Bir Tamiz must have been in use for a very long time for the ropes for raising the water bags had worn many deep ruts in the sides of the tunnel. The water, visible from where we stood, seemed to be greenish brown. Air bubbles kept coming to the surface and lots of tadpoles were swimming in the somber liquid. That is the drawback of all water collected and stored in basins, cisterns or natural rocky clefts. It is always smelly and often revolting. This is inevitable where flocks came regularly to drink and where no protecting wall is built around the mouth of the well. The surroundings of the Arabian watering places are saturated with urine and covered with a layer of caked excrement. Even our Awamir companions seemed to dislike the Bir Tamiz water although they praised its reliability.

Two Beduin meet with the traditional nose-kiss. The greeting will always be: 'What is the news?' 'The news is good, thanks be to God!'

Hunting is a favorite pastime of wealthy desert sheiks. Sheik Isa's prize hunting falcon has earned a reputation for ferocity.

The Beduin women of the desert are freer than their city sisters and do not always wear the veil, but are still inferior to their men.

We had reached our most northerly limit. Longingly our glances traveled to the far horizon which disclosed nothing of what was behind it. We looked out over an endless monotonous rocky plain. Close by, the twisting wadis were visible as they cut out in the plain their steep, crumbling rifts. Further away was a mutilated plain, on the shiny stone surface of which the noonday sun beat mercilessly.

Years later I would get the chance to travel from the northern borderland into that invisible interior, the real Bahr as-Safi – 'sea of pure sand'. Then I stood on the borders of two wide craters in the sand, marked off by lots of pieces of black slag. They are meteorite craters, not the ruins of old towns. This is the land of eternal silence only broken by the sound of the wheezing sands blown by the wind over the sharp edges of the huge hills of pure reddish sand. All other motion, all animal and human life was absent. There was the real Empty Quarter.

Standing on the southern border we were still sur-

As the sun sets on the desert, elongated shadows fall on ever-changing sand formations; men must hurry home before dark.

rounded by animal life and by a sparse vegetation. Here Arabs lived with their flocks, thanks to the milk these animals produced and, as a great exception, thanks to their roasted meat. We resolutely decided to turn our backs on that endless, monotonous Empty Quarter, hoping to meet some families of the tribe that had obeyed its timeless law, hurrying towards drinkable water.

Water, drinkable water, was the first problem. At long last the guide spotted water. It was a pool of drained rainwater. The water was green and covered with a sheet of camel droppings that had swollen in the water till they were like mellow plums. The guide knelt on the edge and with prudent motion of his hand freed a place from the floating plums, then scooped out some of the brown-green water in the hollow of his hand and tasted it attentively. He did this several times. Then, after sighing an *al hamd u lillah* (praise be to Allah) he looked up into our anxious faces and said 'It is fine water'. 'It is no water', we replied, 'it is diluted urine and a brew of dung'. The camels were brought, and for them too the dirt floating on the surface was brushed aside and they

On the empty horizons camels, ships of the desert, can travel for days without food or water, living off their humps.

This woman's mask-like veil not only protects her honor from the eyes of strangers, but also her skin from the sun and the desert winds.

drank some mouthfuls and turned away. Although nearly dying of thirst we neither dared nor could drink this water.

Our small caravan went on, traveling as fast as we could. We found water, the first well with living water we had seen in the Awamir country. A day later we met a Beduin family. There had recently been abundant rain here and one of our men knew a place where a pool of fresh water used to be formed. He was right, and while he stepped forward into the water to fill our water-bags a man and some women came along for a talk. Here was an entirely unexpected desert idyll. The people had no fear because I was alone with one guide, who was their friend. We followed the women to the family dwelling place. Under an overhanging rock a stable had been made for the young and still-delicate goats. The people themselves lived in front of the stable on a flat piece of rock. At night time the starlit sky was their roof and during the day when the heat of the sun burned fiercely, they spanned a woven cloth of black goat's hair over some sticks.

It was early when we approached their home the family was still gathered in the morning sun around the remains of their meal. There were two elderly men, two women, a grown-up son and two children. Some goat's milk and butter milk had been left in wooden bowls. I was warmly invited to join them and gladly I accepted a long drink. How good it tasted. I distributed among the children some biscuits I had left in my pocket. They kept them prudently in their hands and only dared to taste the unknown food when their parents had answered their questioning looks with an affirmative nod. The men did not smoke. The family practically lived by its flock. Occasionally they got some dates or flour, but the principal food of both adults and children was milk, white cheese and the indispensable bitter coffee, made from the husks of coffee beans. I was, of course, offered this Arabian drink of hospitality but I far preferred their butter milk.

Men can live for months on end almost solely on milk and the products made from it. We met people of the southern and western borders of the Empty Quarter who did it; they were lean but looked healthy. In the western borderland we even met men with their camel herd who lived without drinkable water. They had wells but these gave salty bitter water. The camels could drink it and the men drank camel's milk. When they saw us coming they ran towards us with hands in front of their mouths, palms turned upwards like cups, heads turned backward and with imploring eyes. They were imitating drinking. The only gift they asked was drinkable, sweet water, *rahmat Ullahi*, Allah's mercy.

People of Israel

A small minority of Orthodox extremists occasionally disrupt daily life in Israel with often violent demands for stricter religious legislation.

The story of Israel is one of the most astonishing dramas of our time. When the Jewish state became independent in 1948, it had a population of about 800,000 of whom some 650,000 were Jews and 150,000 Arabs. In 1973, 25 years later, the Jews had grown in number to 2·75 million and the Arabs to 480,000. During that period 1·5 million Jews had immigrated into the country; they spoke many different languages and brought many different cultural traditions. Most were destitute, lacking in education and technical skills. They had to be provided with housing and employment,

Under the shade of an old tree Jewish and Arab workers find refuge from the heat of the day and relax together over cups of thick Turkish coffee.

(Right) The Arabs of the West Bank, now under Israeli rule, live much as they did before. Near Nablus an Arab shepherd leads his flocks to the well.

One of the last of his kind, this Yemeni *sofer stam* (scribe) copies the Bible by hand with a goose feather dipped in special pine-cone ink.

medical care and a reasonable standard of living. They had to be taught a new language and re-socialized in a new culture. All this had to be done in a semi-desolate land and amidst the grave threat to the very existence of the new state from the neighboring countries.

Problems of another kind were created by internal schisms within the Jewish population itself. One such schism emerged between the relatively established people and the steady stream of newcomers. Inevitably the established Israelis regarded the newcomers as a threat to their employment, to the resources of their country and their general standard of living, a conflict which was heightened by the generous assistance given by the government to newcomers.

Another internal schism ran on broad ethnic lines, for nearly half the immigrants hailed from Western countries while the other half came from Arab countries. This division into Oriental (Sephardi) and Occidental (Ashkenazi) Jews was deepened by cultural, educational, technological, social and ritual differences. Then a third schism lay between orthodox and non-orthodox Jews. Israel is officially a Jewish state, but the overwhelming majority of its population is not religious and resents the dictates of the rabbis in such matters as transport on the Sabbath, the definition of Jewishness and marriage. This schism is translated into political terms with the for-

Some Orthodox Jews spend their entire lives studying the Bible. Supposedly guardians of the nation's morals, they are exempt from army service.

The Wailing Wall has been the focus of Jewish thoughts and sentiment for centuries. It symbolized suffering. Today it also symbolizes salvation.

mation of religious political parties, ranging from the most fanatically orthodox to the religiously liberal.

Yet today the Israelis present a highly integrated society with a stable and viable institutional system and a distinct culture, a society advanced in the sciences and technology, art and literature, music and drama. And the question that immediately poses itself is how was this possible within such a brief period and against such a background?

The Israelis share a history and an ideology that go back thousands of years to an idealized golden past, when their ancestors achieved independent statehood in the 'Land of Israel' and developed a cultural and spiritual civilization from which Christianity later emanated. The chronicles of that ancient past have been immortalized in the texts of the Old Testament of the Bible and in the Jewish religious traditions. Throughout the long and dark centuries of exile and dispersion following the invasions of their country and the destruction of its spiritual symbol, the Temple in Jerusalem, those traditions and the messianic promise of the return to the 'homeland' were kept alive by daily rituals and ceremonials. They were made perpetually meaningful through ceaseless experiences of discrimination, persecution and pogroms in many parts of the diaspora.

During the 19th century the persecution of Jews in

Though Israel's *raison d'être* is to provide sanctuary for Jews, there is complete freedom of worship for all religious denominations.

Eastern Europe, and particularly in tsarist Russia, reached a new pitch. As a result of this and also of the wave of nationalism which swept through Europe, a Jewish nationalist movement arose whose aim was the actual return to the Holy Land and the resurrection of the Jewish state.

Perhaps the greatest impetus to this movement came in the wake of the holocaust in Europe when, during World War II, nearly 6 million Jews were put to death without any nation making any special effort to save them. This experience created a deep wound, not only in the survivors in Europe – most of whom eventually went to Israel – but in all Jews. The Israelis are convinced that they, and only they, can protect themselves from a similar catastrophe. Every Israeli Jew, no matter where he came from, sees himself as a survivor of the centuries of persecution. No understanding of the modern Israelis is possible if the depth of this experience and the burden of the memories of the past, both remote and recent, are not fully appreciated.

The past is enshrined in the present in every walk of life in Israel. One of the most passionately pursued 'sports' of the contemporary Israelis is archaeology, digging up the past. This is a truly national hobby and is of great political significance. Every discovery of relics of the past becomes a link across the centuries. The people dig for their past to establish their identity in the present. And everywhere in the country the archaeological discoveries become institutionalized as centers for 'pilgrimage' by schoolchildren, youth movements, army units, other Israelis and Jews from abroad. The Dead Sea Scrolls, the oldest Biblical texts in existence, have been placed in the most central area in the capital, Jerusalem, not far from the House of Parliament, the Tomb of Herzel, the Hebrew University and other national establishments. They are housed in a modern domed building which in itself is a piece of creative art. Another archaeological monument that has become a center of national pilgrimage and a stage for massive ceremonials is the top of Masada overlooking the Dead Sea, where over 2,000 years ago a group of militant Jewish zealots made a last stand against the conquering Romans and, after a long siege, drew lots and slew one another in a systematic act of mass suicide to avoid surrender and captivity.

The study of biblical texts and of history generally is systematically combined with the study of the ecology and topography of the country. Every valley, every hill, every part of the country is identified in terms of historical and archaeological associations. Schoolchildren, youth organizations, army units and scholars tour the country from end to end and 'read' their history into the sites. History, land and people all become meaningfully related in the contemporary situation. Themes from more recent history are also introduced into the ancient landscape. Exhibitions of various representations of the

(Over Page) Members of the Eastern Catholic churches crowd the Basilica of the Holy Sepulchre in Jerusalem for their Easter celebrations.

holocaust are permanently established in many parts of the country. Forests are called after extinct Jewish European communities, and everywhere memorials, statues and plaques remind the new Israeli generation of the catastrophe. In some places symbols of the more recent past, of the struggle for independence, are added to those of earlier times.

For the modern Israelis the experience of the holocaust is injected with a fearsome reality in the contemporary situation. Israel has been in a state of war with her neighbors during her entire existence. In 1948 the Arab countries, rejecting a United Nations resolution to partition Palestine between Jews and Arabs, unleashed their armed forces in an attempt to obliterate the newly established Jewish state. Their efforts failed and an armistice was arranged by the United Nations. In the process a large number of Arabs, who had lived in what became Israel, were turned into refugees in neighboring countries – and this exacerbated the issue immensely. Tension continued as the Arab countries regularly declared their resolute intention of destroying 'the Zionist State' and throwing the Jews into the sea. Even after the Six Day War of 1967, when many Arabs discovered that their intention was far-fetched, the Arab League met in Khartoum and passed a unanimous decision – no recognition of Israel, no negotiations with Israel and no peace with Israel.

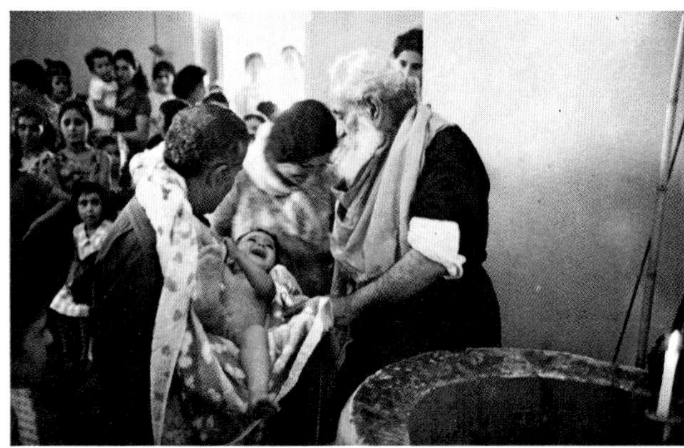

(Top) Born to Christian parents this child is welcomed into their church. He will grow up alongside children of all Jerusalem's other faiths.

There is no civil marriage in Israel. Members of each religious community must be married by their own priests.

This stunning bridal headdress was brought to Israel by the Jews of Yemen who were flown over in the 1950s. It was called 'Operation Magic carpet'.

Many Christians make pilgrimages to the holy places in Israel: the Grotto of the Nativity in Bethlehem attracts many at Christmas.

The Israelis do not dismiss Arab threats as mere propaganda slogans. They believe that the Arabs mean literally what they declare. The holocaust of World War II was carried out by one of Europe's most advanced nations, and Israelis see no reason to doubt their neighbors' declared intentions. Acts of violence across the borders and three major wars have been fought between the two sides since that time, and the estrangement and animosity are now greater than ever before. The state of war – or of 'no peace, no war' as it is sometimes called – is part of the day to day reality; the Israelis have completely adjusted their life and institutions to it.

There is nothing like a common threat to survival to unite a people. Survival is the one basic issue which unites all Israelis despite their social, cultural, religious and political differences. Even the young, opposed to the now old pioneering generation, antagonized by religion and disliking the old slogans and ideologies, are drawn into this elementary condition about which there is no dispute.

Israeli men are conscripted to the Israel Defense Forces at the age of 18, and three years later they become reservists who are called up regularly until they are 55. Women are similarly conscripted, though for shorter periods. The army is truly a people's army with only a small core of professionals who tend to retire early. There is no strict or formal discipline in the army; even the most senior officers are called by their first names by the men, and saluting is rare. There are few signs of militarism in the country: through their long and bitter experiences in countries of exile in the past, the Israelis have developed an acute distrust of regimentation.

Internal divisions and conflicts are also counterbalanced by basic egalitarian tendencies in the distribution of both economic and political power. The disparities in income between the skilled and unskilled, between employer and employee, manager and worker are among the lowest in the liberal world. Wages are not just based on productivity and experience, but also on 'social points' like the number of dependents, state of health and so on. By far the most powerful institution in Israel is the Histadrut, the General Federation of Labor, within which the various Trade Unions are incorporated. A wage earner is first a member of the general organization and only then a member of the Trade Union. The Histadrut also runs industrial, agricultural and financial concerns which constitute a substantial part of the country's total economy. Its associated agricultural settlements – the *kibbutzim* and the *moshavim* – produce the bulk of the agricultural products of the country.

The Histadrut dominates the country in many ways and Israel cynics sometimes refer to its imposing head-

Agricultural festivals replace religious ones in many communal settlements. The first harvest is especially joyous and there is dancing in the fields.

quarters in Tel Aviv as the Kremlin. Largely through its influence in all these fields, however, it has achieved a high standard of living for the Israeli worker and ensured an even distribution of incomes. Israel is also very much a welfare state, providing for the unemployed, the bereaved and the needy, paying child and maternity allowances and pensions.

Education in Israel is compulsory and free from the age of five to fifteen. There are seven institutions of higher learning and advanced research in the country, including the Hebrew University in Jerusalem, the Weizman Institute of Science in Rehovot and the Technion in Haifa. There are many other institutions of medical, scientific and technological research; these include two atomic reactors.

The mineral wells of the Dead Sea are known for their therapeutic qualities. Young and old enjoy mud bathes at the lowest point on earth.

(Centre) Each Easter Friday the cross is borne along the famous Via Dolorosa in Old Jerusalem by local Christians and pilgrims.

At prayer, Orthodox Jews wear *teffilin*: small boxes containing sacred scrolls held to the hand and forehead by a winding black strap.

Egalitarianism in incomes is more than matched by equality in political rights within a parliamentary democratic system based on the principle of one man, one vote. Pressure from outside and the need for a great deal of centralized planning and controls would, under normal circumstances, have led to an increasing authoritarianism. But the Israelis are notoriously partisan. As the saying goes 'two Israelis make three parties'. Power in the country is fragmented and jealously decentralized. The electoral system that the state adopted enhances and perpetuates these very things. In Israel the leaders are austere, highly idealistic and singularly lacking in personal wealth.

Sharing the same historical tradition and destiny, standing together in the face of external threat, and living under the same economic and political institutions have inevitably led to the development of a new Israeli culture, combining old symbols and new symbols within a new integrated culture. The Israelis speak Hebrew, the ancient language of the Bible, which is now the only *lingua franca* in the country. A humorist once remarked: 'Israel is the only country in the world where a mother learns the mother tongue from her children'. For a long time this has been to some extent true, as the children of immigrants learnt Hebrew in school and imparted it to their parents at home. Although the language has kept its basic grammatical structure, it has been highly redeveloped and revitalized by sustained and systematic efforts on the part of specialist bodies who continually meet to coin new words for new categories and concepts and who regularly distribute specialized lexicons throughout the country. A good many words from English and from other European languages have been incorporated.

Like many other Mediterranean peoples, the Israelis live mainly out of doors, on balconies, beaches, parks and the sides of streets. People talk to strangers in a familiar fashion on buses, trains and in the streets, tell jokes and sing amidst all the tensions and difficulties of their world.

With a few exceptions, all non-Jewish Israelis speak Arabic as their first language. But they are far from being a homogenous group: they are sharply divided on religious lines. About 70 per cent are Muslims, 20 per cent Christians and 10 per cent Druzes. These religious groups are highly autonomous; they run their own places of worship and their own courts regulating matters of personal status like marriage and divorce. In the latter case, however, Israeli legislation has brought women equality and thus imposed some limitations on the jurisdiction of these courts. This has particularly affected Islamic family law since it prohibits polygyny and it gives women equal rights in custody over children and any inheritance.

The Christians are divided into many denominations; the largest in numbers are the Greek Orthodox and the Latin and Greek Catholics. The Druzes (see pages 84-85) who had been a persecuted minority sect almost all over the Muslim world, were for the first time officially recognized as an autonomous religious community in Israel, with their own religious organization and courts.

Arab Beduin in Israel are fast becoming settled and the overwhelming majority of Arab villagers now work in Jewish towns and settlements to which they commute daily. And the fast growing cities are sprawling in all directions with the result that many Arab villages are also becoming suburbs of Jewish towns. Arab settlements have their own local and municipal councils; their own schools in which the children learn in Arabic, and where Hebrew is used only as a second language at a later stage in the curriculum. With equal work opportunities from the Histadrut, the Arabs in Israel have achieved a high standard of living.

Yet the Arabs are politically insecure. They find themselves in a precarious position because of the wider political conflict between Israel and the Arab countries. The Jews in Israel suspect their loyalties, and the Arabs across the borders often look on them as renegades. They cannot fight against the Jewish state, and they cannot become fully integrated within it. And the more material benefits they gain from living within Israel, the more dependent they become on the country. Frequently they ask the question expressed in their poetry and novels, 'Who are we? Arabs? Israelis?'

Paradoxically enough the Jews in Israel, when they can afford to reflect, pose similar questions about the nature of their own identity. What are we? Jews? But many of us are not religious and yet we say we are Jews? Who is a Jew anyway? By what criterion is Jewishness measured? The rabbis say that a Jew must be the child of a Jewish woman and according to Jewish law, children of a Jewish man and a non-Jewish woman are not Jews; yet these may know no other identity than Judaism; they are conscripted to the army and speak Hebrew as their first language. Some of the politicians on the other hand maintain that a Jew is a person who identifies himself with Judaism and with Jewish history. But the orthodox retort that this is hardly a clear criterion and point out the dangers to the very identity of the state if the stricter definition of a Jew is not adopted.

Many Israelis try to avoid these issues by stressing that they are Israelis, bearers of Israeli citizenship and culture. But this raises the same questions and creates similar dilemmas. Who is an Israeli? A citizen of Israel? If that is so, then there should be no difference between Jews and Arabs within the country. But in that case the whole *raison d'etre* of the state will be undermined. This will inevitably lead to the severance of the links between Israel and its most faithful and true ally – the Jewish people abroad who, during all these years, have materially and morally supported Israel. Many other Israelis, both Jewish and Arab, trust hopefully that these problems of identity will become academic when peace comes to the Holy Land.

People of Oman

The traditional way of life of the people of Oman has been very largely influenced by the physical features of their country – the sea, the mountains and the desert. Oman is virtually an island, surrounded on two sides by ocean and on the other two by an even more formidable sea – the billowing sands of the Rub al Khali. Its people are noted among Europeans for their religious fervor and suspicion of their fellow men.

Some three quarters of a million people live in this well-watered region of south-east Arabia. Yet even though there is a strong regional sense among the inhabitants of this island of settlement called Oman, it has rarely been politically united during its long and well-documented history. Today it is divided into eight putative states. The most important of the internal divisions is that between the seven states of Trucial Oman – Abu Dhabi, Dubai, Ras al-Khailmah, Ajman, Umm al-Qaiwain, Sharjah and Fujairah, now loosely federated into the Union of Arab Emirates – and the Sultanate of Oman, known until recently as the Sultanate of Muscat and Oman.

For those living on the coast fishing plays a major part

A camel driver in Muscat carries a stick to guide the camels. His companion, a desert tribesman, has a more lethal weapon.

Built with the help of newly discovered oil, a modern school replaces the old village Koran schools for boys in Oman.

Behind the mud brick walls of houses separated by narrow alleys, Muslim families live private secluded lives away from the eyes of strangers.

in the local economy. At the beginning of the year fishermen net small fish, mostly sardines and anchovies, close to the shore. It is not until the risk of winter storms has finally gone that they venture out in their boats to catch the larger predators. Large numbers of the fish caught are dried and exported. The main fishing season only lasts for half the year. Fortunately for the Omani on the Batina coast the seasonally limited fishing is not their only source of livelihood. Nearly all along the Batina coast the villagers cultivate date palms, fruits such as bananas, oranges and lemons and vegetables and a few cereals. This is possible because there is an ample supply of water from wells which reach fresh water draining from the mountains to the sea. On the Persian Gulf, however, there is no fresh water and the people cannot cultivate crops. Instead, until the collapse of the natural pearl market in the 1930s, the people living on this coast went pearling.

At the beginning of June every single able-bodied man on the Trucial coast would join the fleets which left the main ports for the pearl banks in the shallow waters of the lower gulf. There the boats remained for about two and a half months. Life aboard the boats was incredibly tough. The divers, existing in the torrid heat on fetid water and a handful of fish, dates and rice, would descend to five and twelve fathoms forty, fifty, even sixty times a day returning with small bagfulls of oysters. When the day's diving was over there was more work to be done. The whole crew would start opening the pile of stinking shells, always in the hope that they would find a pearl of great price which would free them from the mire of debt that kept them enslaved to this wretched life. Not one of the crew received a basic wage: every man, from the ship's cook to the merchant who sold the pearls on the Bombay market, depended for his profits on the hazards of the catch and the whim of the international market. But while the big merchants could spread their investments and in any case took a larger share of the profits, the men whose job was looking for the pearls received only a share of the proceeds of their individual boat. Often they did not earn even sufficient to pay back the advances they took in order that their families could eat while they were at sea. So the crews owed money to their captains, the ship owners to the intermediary merchants and the small traders to the big dealers. For the poor there was little hope of ever getting out of debt. When a man could no longer work another member of his family had to replace him. There can be few who actually experienced the conditions of pearling that today regret its passing.

In addition to the natural resources of fish and pearls the sea also brought considerable wealth to some Omani in the form of a share in the maritime trade which passed between the Indian Ocean and the Mediterranean, Arab and Persian worlds via the Persian Gulf. Particularly important for them were the contacts with East Africa. The special relationship between the two areas survived the suppression of slavery and the disruption of traditional trading patterns brought about by European commercial and imperial interests in the 19th century. A collateral branch of the Al Bu Sa'id Sultans of Muscat continued to rule in Zanzibar until 1964 and despite the events of independence Omani are still to be found living in Tanzania.

The interior of Oman is isolated and the people who live there tend to be tribal and inward looking. Cut off from contact with the other inhabited parts of the Arabian peninsula by the Empty Quarter the population of the mountains has itself condensed into little nuclei of fortified settlements within the deeply entrenched valleys. There are no large towns; the population of the biggest settlements, Nizwa, Rustaq and Sumayil, do not exceed eight thousand.

The livelihood of the villagers is based on the cultivation of dates which they sell. They also cultivate other fruits, particularly lemons, oranges and bananas, and alfalfa to supplement the natural grazing of the village livestock – sheep, goats, cows and donkeys. The sup-

Omani gun-vendors do a good trade. Most men carry guns but rarely use them, in spite of guerrilla warfare to the south in the province of Dhofar.

The governor of Ibri surrounded by his armed guards. Each province has a governor who represents the Sultan and metes out justice.

plementary seasonal winter flow of the irrigation system is used to grow a variety of grain and vegetable crops. The water supply of these agricultural communities is remarkable. An aquifer is tapped near the foot of the mountains and the water is brought to the surface by means of an underground gallery. These galleries (*falaj*) are usually five to seven miles long and 60 feet deep at the mother well. This technique of mining water is Persian in origin and the building of the network of *falaj* in Oman goes right back to pre-Islamic times when Oman belonged to the Persian Achamaenid and Sassanid monarchies. High in the Jabal Akhdhar, which rise to 10,000 feet, the date palm cannot grow and the villagers here cultivate exotic fruits: peaches, apricots, walnuts, pomegranates. They also tend roses from which they make rose-water to sell as perfume.

In addition to the settled villagers who make up the majority of the population of interior Oman there are also the nomadic groups, the Bedu of the desert fringes and the Shawawi of the mountains. The Bedu herd goats, sheep and camels in the savanna country along the western foot of the mountains. Here they also own and cultivate palms. The Bedu migrate seasonally. In the winter they move out with their flocks into the desert to seek fresh grazing. In the summer they retreat onto the permanent wells of the piedmont zone. The Bedu who only herd camels, however, tend to move into the sand desert where a limited supply of water can be found in the dunes.

Within the mountains the Shawawi also move seasonally from the lowlands around the villages in the valleys to the high plateau settlements, mostly on the edge of the Jabal Akhdhar massif. The Jabal Akhdhar, the Green Mountain is the central peak of a range which extends unbroken for 400 miles from the Persian Gulf to the Indian Ocean. Their name is inappropriate since the slopes and precipices are as bare and barren as the land around. The Shawawi nomads usually have extremely close relationships with the settled villagers.

The patterns of traditional life in Oman are changing with extraordinary speed thanks to the new wealth brought by oil.

It was not until the beginning of the 1960s that oil was discovered in commercial quantities, first in Abu Dhabi, the largest of the Trucial Sheikdoms by area, and then in the Sultanate of Oman where exports started in 1967. Now the state of Dubai has also joined the oil producers with a small offshore field.

The fact that Oman was the last part of the Gulf in which oil was discovered has cost the region dear. Already denuded of its traditional crafts, commerce and overseas possessions as a result of the impact of European trading and political interests, the basic agricultural economy also began to flounder in the years following World War II as the active working population began to leave the country to seek employment in the new oil-rich states further up the Gulf. This exodus was accelerated by an internal civil war which resulted in the unification of Muscat and Oman under the repressive régime of a Sultan who managed to stay in office until 1970. Some of the exiles are now returning home with skills that are useful for the country but with political ideas that might be considered by the government as less so.

The actual occurrence of oil discoveries has also upset the old balance in the region for the oil fields are in the sparsely populated desert fringes away from the populated core of the mountains and east coast. This means that a major redistribution of wealth has occurred. Furthermore the Sultanate has to bear the brunt of an expensive war in its southern Dhofar province against the 'Popular Front for the Liberation of the Arabian Gulf' which is fighting to overthrow all the régimes in the oil-rich Gulf. This revolt, despite British military help, consumes 60 per cent of the Omani budget.

Today Oman is in a state of fundamental revolution. Gone forever are the days of tribal rule and the isolation of the interior. Gone too, almost certainly is the possible hope of a peaceful integration of the area, particularly since Britain has withdrawn her centripetal presence

The fish market is not always well stocked. Fishing is seasonal and for six months fishermen become farmers or pearl divers.

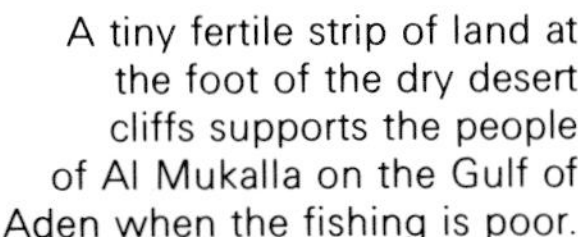

A tiny fertile strip of land at the foot of the dry desert cliffs supports the people of Al Mukalla on the Gulf of Aden when the fishing is poor.

Girls begin wearing jewelry and cosmetics as babies. Black kohl enlarges and protects the eyes and ocher paste guards the skin from the fierce desert sun.

Since the 1960s oil has brought vast wealth to some. A game of golf and a 'saloon', instead of a common jeep, are coveted status symbols.

The faithful are summoned to pray from the minarets rising above San'a in north Yemen. Worthiness in the eyes of God is every man's goal.

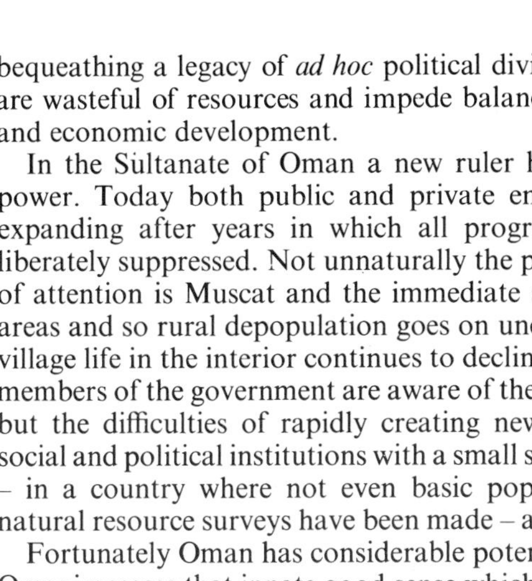

bequeathing a legacy of *ad hoc* political divisions which are wasteful of resources and impede balanced regional and economic development.

In the Sultanate of Oman a new ruler has come to power. Today both public and private enterprise are expanding after years in which all progress was deliberately suppressed. Not unnaturally the present focus of attention is Muscat and the immediate surrounding areas and so rural depopulation goes on unchecked and village life in the interior continues to decline. The wiser members of the government are aware of these problems but the difficulties of rapidly creating new economic, social and political institutions with a small state revenue – in a country where not even basic population and natural resource surveys have been made – are immense.

Fortunately Oman has considerable potential and the Omani possess that innate good sense which goes with a long history of national development. Whether these advantages prove adequate to survive the stresses of creating the new state remains to be seen. On its success or otherwise depends not only the future of Oman but also the political stability of the Gulf and the future of the developed world's energy supplies.

All Omani men carry a silver dagger. They are very expensive but the more ornate the dagger, the greater the wearer's prestige.

Oman today is virtually in a state of revolution brought about by rapid oil-accelerated progress and disintegration of traditional peasant life.

To satisfy the requirements of their religion, the Omanis must always cut the throats of livestock which they butcher for food.

Women behind the veil

The Arab world

Strict Islamic religious law requires that a woman conceal her body but it does not demand that her face be covered. But in some countries where veiling is most strictly practised custom demands that a woman wears a cloth mask over her face through the whole of her waking hours in addition to the veil she draws down over it if she leaves the house. In places like Dubai and Abu Dhabi, where the governments have used oil revenues to encourage modernization and social life is changing rapidly, one notices that the eye holes in the mask are growing bigger and the bottom of the mask, which used to descend below the chin, is now up to the mouth, while the enveloping veil is made of flimsier material.

This is one example of wide changes in the status of women which have been in progress for the last 50 years. They are the result of wider contacts with the outside world combined with reformist movements and modern education. Many reformists regarded the veil as both a symbol and a cause of backwardness, but it was thought to be a matter too sensitive for legislation. The veil is not only connected with women's subordination to men but with ideas of family honor and feminine modesty. Rather than abolishing the veil by decree, as was done in Egypt in 1920 and in Iran in 1935, reformists in Arab countries and Turkey simply left the veil to pass out of fashion. It has done so more completely in the cities, particularly in the Mediterranean area, than it has in remote areas and the strongholds of religious conservatism such as Saudi Arabia.

In the old days towns were the very places where veiling was practised most strictly, especially among the more prosperous classes. It went with a whole way of life in which, for reasons of modesty and family respectability, women were expected to live in seclusion, seeing little of anyone outside the family and a few women visitors. In the desert Beduin life did not permit these conventions. Beduin women are always ready to talk to strangers and travelers and even to provide them with hospitality when their men are away with the herds.

The strict code of seclusion forbids women to have any but the briefest and most superficial contact with men other than their husbands and kinsmen too closely related to marry them. A woman is said to be 'forbidden' even in death. In some places a woman's corpse is concealed in a double shroud (coffins are not used) and committed to the grave under the further concealment of a canopy. Only close kinsmen carry the bier of a dead woman, whereas it is regarded as a pious act to help carry the bier of a Muslim man, even a stranger. When a famous man dies his bier is sometimes passed from hand to hand by men lining the whole route to the cemetery. A 19th century orientalist commented on the fact that men were even forbidden to enter the tombs of the Prophet's wives and other women of his family in the holy city of Medina. In Cairo the bodies of men and women were never buried in the same vault unless separated by a wall.

The code of seclusion has influenced the design of houses. Only if it has upper storeys does a traditional house have windows in the outside walls. Ground floor windows open onto an inner courtyard and there is usually a curtain wall built inside the doorway so that passers-by cannot see in from the street.

The customs of seclusion strongly accentuate the contrast between public and private life, a contrast which affects men almost as much as women. Whereas men go to the mosque at least on Fridays, in many parts of the Arab world women pray only at home. In the market, where the shopping is mostly done by men, and in other public places men lead a gregarious social life in which family matters are usually not discussed. If a man wants to know what is happening in his friend's family he will often have to ask his wife who will have heard the news from his friend's wife or sister. Religious precept requires women to obey their husbands, but even in traditional society older women can be very powerful figures in the home. It is commonly the wife who looks after family money among poorer people.

Women usually visit each other in the daytime when the men are out. In the more traditional places the women of a household pay such visits in groups, not only for company but to chaperon each other in the streets. Modesty requires women to be extremely careful about the moral reputation of women outside the family whom they admit to their house or whose houses they visit. In any case, too much visiting is frowned upon.

A woman's reputation for chastity is part of the honor of her whole family. If she falls into disgrace not only does her family lose esteem, but also the sons' and daughters' chances of making good marriages are reduced. In more tribally oriented countries, the code of honor permitted – and even encouraged – brothers and paternal cousins to kill a girl who had compromised the family honor.

In traditional Arab life, women have suffered from considerable social and economic disabilities. Until recently in the Gulf states it was unusual even for wealthy families to teach their women to read and write. A woman could not go out to work to support herself, or her dependents if she had any, whatever the circumstances of hardship because it would mean making contact with men from outside the family.

Until modern reforms husbands could divorce their wives at will with a minimum of official formality. It was, and still is, extremely difficult for a wife to divorce her husband. The ease of divorce can sometimes have ironical consequences. A man may divorce his wife in a fit of pique and then have to give her a substantial present to persuade her to remarry him. It is also customary for a wife to be given such a present to persuade her to accept an additional wife. Islam permits a man to marry up to

It is not religious law but custom which decrees that a woman veil her face. Only very gradually is modern life unveiling Muslim women.

four wives. He must treat them equally and is expected to provide them at the very least with separate rooms if not separate establishments. But only a minority of marriages have ever been polygamous and secular law often now discourages or forbids them.

In the more traditional of Arab towns and villages a girl's first marriage is arranged by her parents when she is not much past puberty. She joins her husband in his household and, unless her husband is an older man, that will usually be her father-in-law's house. There she must answer not only to her husband but to her new set of parents as well, especially her mother-in-law.

Even today a woman's greatest security lies in her children and particularly in her sons. Her failure to bear a son can easily lead to divorce. If she is divorced or widowed her sons are under a strong obligation to look after her even if they are quite young. So long as she has a son, a woman's secluded helplessness can to a limited degree become her strength. A man who divorces his son's mother runs the risk of losing the son as well, who will be obliged to go and set up house for his mother. But there is little in traditional life to mitigate the difficulties of childless older women. For them seclusion behind the veil can mean great unhappiness.

People of Egypt

Over a thousand years old, the great university mosque of Al-Azhar is the focal point of political and religious life in Cairo.

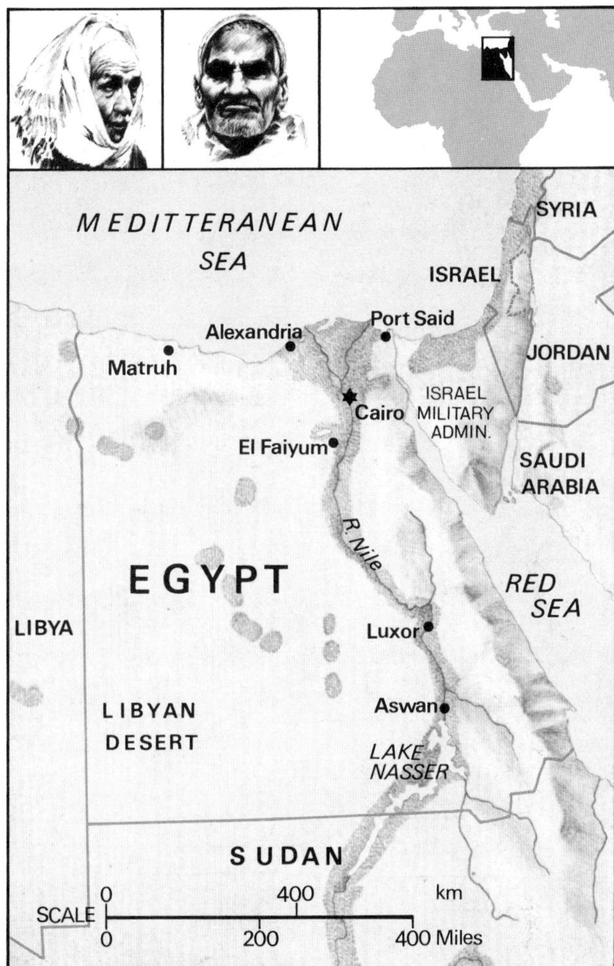

Egypt, say its people, is the mother of the world. Distinctive, continuous, always itself, even the word conveys far more than any mere name. A narrow green valley laid in a wide waste of desert. The vast slow river Nile spreads its waters into a thousand channels over the earth it has itself brought down, before it fans out into the flat reaches of the delta. The boundary between the sands and rich soil, between civilization and emptiness, is as thin as a knife blade. The river has created everything in Egypt: time, space, land and people. It has given Egypt an immediate unique identity. Even now, when so much of the world has become indistinguishable from the rest, to go to Egypt is to become a traveler again, to have accomplished something real, to have experienced something different.

But precisely because the Nile and the country have so evocative a hold on the imagination we must be careful not to think of Egypt only as a mysterious and timeless world. We need to know the human reality, not the vague dream of an unchanging peasantry who plant and harvest the passing years.

To begin with, only a tiny area of the huge space

With a population of over 6 million, Cairo is one of the most crowded cities in the world. All of Egypt is controlled from here.

within the country's borders is habitable. In comparison to most other areas of the Middle East this small part of Egypt is densely populated. Its 37 million people are funneled into the thin strip of the Nile valley and the settlements in the desert oases to the west. These people have been dominated since earliest times by a high civilization and a centralized government which controlled the vital irrigation system. They have a relatively efficient but still very low level of technology, and are dependent above all on agriculture. It is small wonder that the Egyptians seem to be very much one people, with one culture and one character.

Classically 'Egyptians' means the *fellahin*, the peasantry and the agricultural laborers. Over the centuries they have been ruled by Persians, Greeks, Romans, Byzantines, Arabs (Arabic is still the spoken language of all the population), Turks, French and English. These rulers have commanded their labor, taken their men for armies, extracted taxes, rent and the surplus fruits of their labor for governments of which the peasants have never been a part, in towns few of them have ever seen. Yet the *fellahin* remain when their masters have disappeared. Their way of life has survived all the changes of language, religion and history. Even many Beduin tribes, for so long a political threat living on the desert margins of society, were eventually absorbed into the *fellahin* in the 19th century while their leaders became landowners. Outsiders have sometimes seen only passivity or fatalism as the key to peasant resilience. Others, looking closer, have recorded protests and revolts against taxation and forced labor. They have noted too the humor, vigor and realism of Egyptian village life in the midst of grinding poverty. And then they have wondered whether the indifference, the apparent patience and lack of understanding were not in part used as finely-honed weapons against the bureaucrat, the overseer, the landlord and prince.

The villages of the *fellah* lie usually a little way from the river bank, clustering together beneath the palm trees. There are over 4,000 of them scattered through the early mist, canals and flat spaces of lush wet green in the delta, down the valley to Aswan in the south, where the desert and the bleached stony hills press in hard on the fields. They may be any size, from a few hundred people to a few thousand. Raised up slightly on low mounds of earth old dwellings have left behind, the houses seem from a distance to be one, with no distinctive shape or color. Only the elaborate whitewashed dovecotes and the barren cemetery space on waste land to one side have a different aspect. The stranger, walking through the maze of narrow paths between the mud walls, unable to see the interior of any house, will have no sense of plan, no feeling of order.

Yet there is a very complex organization in which descent, family, wealth, property, age and ritual all play their part. It will not be apparent to the eye, but the village is probably divided into quarters by invisible but well-known boundaries. Each quarter is the residence of one or more clans or large descent groups. The families regarded as being of one stock have their links continually renewed by marriage and co-operation in daily tasks. The quarter may have its clan guest house and will share in the great occasions of village life – weddings, funerals, circumcisions, religious festivals and the long social evenings of the holy month of Ramadan. Relations with other groups in the village may also be formalized through marriage, but this will not prevent bitter conflicts arising. Kinship does not guarantee order when clan leaders struggle for local influence.

The stranger will soon learn who these local village leaders are. Some are men who have been able to acquire land and others can claim descent from a saint or holy family. Still others have gained influence over a large descent group by marriage, relative wealth, or by a religious or secular education in the city.

One of these men will have won the contest to be village mayor, or *umda*. This post is easier now than it was 100 years ago when the mayor and local leaders were liable to feel the brunt of government anger over unpaid taxes or failed obligations. At that time the villages were legal, collective units and shared responsibility for the supply of labor and taxes. In Upper (southern) Egypt too the land round the village was redistributed periodically. But after the 1880s taxation became an individual responsibility, more and more land became privately owned and redistribution ceased. Social unity, however, remained only partially eroded by the growth of the rural landowning class. These were notables who acted as local mediators and patrons for the lower peasantry in return for various services. Joined with the villagers in marriage or by shared descent from some founding ancestor, the notables were still 'sons of the village'. Other functionaries were not.

Government agents and landlords' bailiffs were for a long time the unwelcome link with the outside official world. They in turn were often allied to that grim figure of peasant lore all over the world, the moneylender,

When President Nasser died in 1970, roads and railways into Cairo overflowed. Tens of thousands of Egyptians came to pay their last respects.

In the midday heat Cairo businessmen refresh themselves. Some like to smoke their *nargileh*, others prefer the challenge of backgammon.

(Bottom) Sceptical of modern technology, this Cairo car recovery service makes exclusive use of the old reliable donkey.

In the villages of Egypt, life changes little. In the cafés men and boys still perform the erotic pantomime dances of Upper Egypt.

In a country where many women still wear the veil, Maître Moufida Abdul Rahman stands out as a highly respected and well educated lawyer.

In a dark alley in one of Cairo's crowded bazaars a peasant who has come to seek work in the city presses people's clothes.

Zaki, a famous belly dancer and television personality, gives private tutoring to a wealthy pupil in her luxury apartment.

The vendor of *tamarhindi*, a drink made from dates, is a welcome sight on a hot day. His traditional brass urn promises cool refreshment.

The property of many rich Egyptians was confiscated after the fall of King Farouk, but some have managed to retain their wealth and servants.

who was real enough as an agent of family impoverishment. Their other links with the outside world were less threatening: visits to neighboring markets if the village did not have its own shops, traveling traders and artisans, marriage into related groups in the region, the migration of local boys who maintained contact with their families and returned home to marry. These strands were part of a network by which the village was connected to many others. Yet a sense of distinctiveness remains and is carefully preserved. An Egyptian sociologist writing in 1954 of his own village recalled four families of 'strangers'. One family was engaged in carpentry, another in pottery and the repair of utensils, the third were water carriers and the last, a Christian family, ran a cornmill. All these groups lived at different points just outside the village. Although they may have been there for 50 years, playing an important part in the everyday life of the people, they remain 'strangers'.

Most villagers work on the land. Like so many peasant societies across the world they live at a subsistence level and depend on their own family for labor. Each member can and does perform a whole range of tasks in his farming life. Life and work are the same; you do not *work* as a peasant, you *are* a peasant. Increasingly, however, there is a wide range of occupations available. Some go to the towns as laborers, semi-skilled construction workers, waiters, tradesmen, even clerks in small offices if they are literate. Others become craftsmen, passing on their knowledge to their sons, or turn to small shopkeeping. But in most places the land retains its primacy and is still sacred. The *fellah,* whose life is thought of in the towns as a byword of mind-killing drudgery, exalts farming as the noblest and most blessed way of life. He values the land as the highest good. To have to sell your land is not only an economic loss, it is also a social dishonor, a disgrace to your ancestors and a shame and deprivation to your children. If the *fellah* is oppressed by his government, at least he has this intense, organic relationship with the soil on which his whole life depends. He is not merely another man's instrument.

Yet relatively few of the peasantry are independent owners of land. There are no reliable figures, but it may be that as many as three-quarters of the rural population

The British occupation of Egypt ended in 1914, but their legacies, such as the game of croquet, have become a part of the affluent Egyptian's life.

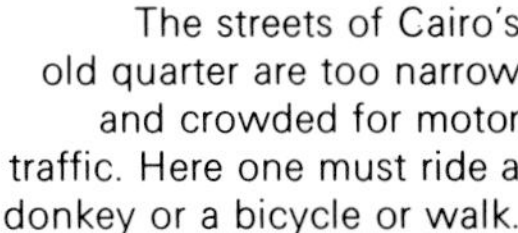

The streets of Cairo's old quarter are too narrow and crowded for motor traffic. Here one must ride a donkey or a bicycle or walk.

were until very recently either completely without land or had not sufficient to provide for their families. Before the revolution of 1952 many of the *fellahin* were little better than serfs in the *izbas* (hamlets) of the estates belonging to the great landowners. Not only the tools but even the houses belonged to the landowner, and most of the livestock too. If they were sharecroppers they might get a quarter of the crop, while the owner provided the animals, seed, and implements. As laborers they had only irregular work for irregular wages, harvesting, road work, cotton picking (particularly in Lower Egypt), canal digging and repairing. The surplus of labor made even migration to the towns insecure. Since 1952 the confiscation of the vast royal and upper-class estates, land redistribution, and the establishment of co-operatives for better farming methods and marketing conditions have improved their lives. But for many rural families land-owning is still a dream, and impermanent wage labor still the reality.

The tools they have to work with are ancient and simple, but effective. The hoe is the basic implement. Together with a cow-drawn plow, a palm trunk or beam

Outside a Coptic church, hearse and driver await the end of the funeral service. Only the very rich can afford a burial like this.

Children owe their father unquestioning obedience and respect. Highly indulged for the first five years of their lives, their childhood then comes to an abrupt end, and they begin working, absorbed into the cycles of the earth. In front of their father they are silent, attentive to his wants. They serve his guests, run errands, obey commands. The older ones dare not smoke in front of him, but sit near the door in the place of least esteem. Between brothers respect for seniority is the rule. Friends are made among one's own age group, not above or below it. As the boys grow up and marry they may still live in the same family compound if there is any land. Gradually the unit gets bigger, and it includes not only their own children but also perhaps a cousin, an old grandmother, orphaned nephews and half brothers or sisters, all living in neighboring rooms. What it is most unlikely to include is a man with two wives: expense and the endless possibility of domestic explosion make polygyny a rare indulgence.

The mother effectively rules the house, as her husband works in the fields. The girls quickly learn to cook, manage accounts and stores and the younger children, draw water and all the other domestic tasks. In Upper Egypt a girl will often go veiled outside and will certainly observe the utmost discretion in public, moving

to level the land and the precious work animals (camels, water buffalo and donkeys) it makes up the technological world of the *fellah*. The hoe is all he requires to grow his main crops – in winter, wheat and barley; in summer, millet with some clover and a few vegetables. When he needs extra water for the fields and has to raise it from the Nile, he uses the water wheel or a bucket lift. Apart from this there are few other aids. There is only a very limited mechanization in the countryside, unless the co-operatives can provide tractors for plowing and chemical fertilizer to replace the nitrous clays or other local substitutes he has been using.

Children, especially sons, are very important in the *fellah*'s life. Male children are highly valued – and a source of much pride – as making a man truly head of his own family. But the boy is also from the age of seven or so a vital source of assistance and free labor, able to take on more and more of the major tasks, until he is 17 and a *fellah* like his father. It is often argued, and rightly, that Egypt's exploding population rate is a terrible burden on a country with limited resources that is trying to modernize. But for the peasant, children are as crucial to his life as his land.

The desert sand is kinder in death than in life. Hot and dry it has preserved this mother and child, silent witnesses to some long-ago tragedy.

The great pyramids attract not only foreign tourists. Many Egyptians travel far to see these remains of their glorious past – and take photos.

quickly along the paths close to the wall, apparently unseen by passing village men. In Lower Egypt and the delta, on the other hand, women work in the fields with men and go unveiled. But everywhere, whatever local differences, the mother is a figure to be respected. Well might she be. For she is the source of the family's good name and honor, the most precious resource of all. Should she or a daughter lose this honor in some village scandal, only a revenge killing can wipe out the stain. Even apart from this honorable role, women are associated with magical powers, with healing and with averting the evil eye.

Of all areas of peasant life perhaps that of the family has been least affected by the changes of the last 50 years. But in many other ways the villages are changing and the customary co-operatives are in decline. Since World War II more and more of the *fellahin* have drifted off the land into the cities or the new industrial towns, compelled by a rising rural population and the miseries of irregular wage labor. Nothing ties them to the land, save another's orders. Those who have stayed, especially the sharecroppers and small land holders, have turned increasingly to cash-crops produced for the ever-growing market rather than the old subsistence crops geared only to family needs. Cotton, sugar beet, vegetables sold to government agencies or in local markets have given a boost to the economy of many villages. Those who prosper show it in brick dwellings next to the mud walls of their neighbors' houses, in their home furnishings that are no longer the simple mats and cushions of the past, even in discarding the flowing *gallabiya* (long outer garment) for more western dress. Communications are better so that visits to the city can be fairly frequent. A son there may now be supplementing his father's income by working in a factory, not gathering fertilizer.

The *fellah* still depends on factors beyond his control – market fluctuations, government planning, even, since the great Aswan Dam began to operate in the late 1960s, the level of the river itself. If that changes, what can remain the same? Coffee houses replace clan gatherings. Folklore and stories of mythical heroes give way to the radio. Hospitality and feast-giving becomes an individual not a group ritual. The young join local football clubs, their elders lament a decline in respect. Money opens a wider door to prestige than descent. The unchanging *fellah* changes.

The vast majority of Egyptians are Sunni, or orthodox, Muslims. That is to say that they believe in the absolute oneness of God and in the mission of His Prophet Mohammed to the community of Muslims. The latter is regarded as the last in a line of prophets which includes Moses and Jesus. This belief, founded on the divine revelation of the Koran, alongside the five pillars of faith – prayer, pilgrimage, almsgiving, holy war and fasting – is the core of Islam. But how do people live according to their beliefs? How significant is it for them in their everyday world? For Islam, like all religions, ultimately depends not only on its central doctrines, but also on the sense and the way ordinary people interpret it in their daily lives.

The great Cairo mosque university of Al-Azhar preserves the teaching of Islam. Here, if anywhere, is the formal center of religion in Egypt. Established over 1,000 years ago (in 942 AD) it has for almost as long been a focal point of the city. From it have graduated the learned men, the sheiks (a word with many meanings: Beduin tribal leader, elder, religious specialist). By their teaching in the traditional Koranic schools they brought some knowledge of the Revelation to the people. To Al-Azhar have come students from all over the Muslim world, from Morocco, even from China, to sit at the feet of sheiks in the great courtyard before returning home to become teachers in their own land. It has guarded the tradition of Islam in law, in theology and in the interpretation of the Holy Book.

Yet Al-Azhar has been far more than a college. It is also a mosque. All mosques are meeting places, vital centers of social life in towns and villages. Each main mosque has its own quarter of which it is a symbol and

(Over page) Within the great walls of the pyramids of Giza the Pharaohs Khufu, Khafre and Menkaure were buried thousands of years ago.

The Nile was a god in Ancient Egypt. It is still the source of life; nearly 40 million *fellahin* work their land along its banks.

Each peasant family must depend on its own labor for survival. Sons are a blessing: from the age of seven they can help to fetch water.

a focus. Men meet there for the daily prayers and for the great public prayers at midday on Friday. They sit and talk beforehand on the rich carpets or simple reed mats; friends greet each other; students wander round memorizing their work or sit against the pillars of the long colonnades; the poor beg alms or stretch out to rest, and the murmur of Koranic recitations is soft beside the chatter of children. The intense communality so characteristic of Islam is concentrated in the mosque.

In times of crisis it is here that people gather, that men seek hospitality, take refuge or prepare to resist oppression. Politics belongs here as much as religion. In the 18th century the sheiks would beat the drum from the minaret of Al-Azhar and summon a crowd of thousands against an unjust prince. Students resisted Napoleon's invasion of 1798; support was proclaimed for the Palestinians in 1948; President Nasser announced the Suez war from the pulpit in 1956, and sermons are regularly filled with political pronouncements. A mosque is popular in the fundamental sense that it is 'of the people' and a part of their everyday lives.

The sheiks (learned men, or *ulema*, as they are called), are not the only men who have religious prestige. Islam is after all without a clergy or body of priests. Though the *ulema* are to be respected for their learning they are not inherently superior to other Muslims. Any man can lead the prayers, even if in the mosques it is usually a sheik. They have no special power to bless, no way of denying a Muslim access to the Divine, no authority to forgive sins, to prescribe penances or bar a man from his worship. The basic egalitarianism of Islam is not corrupted by clericalism. Nevertheless, being a sheik is a profession of high reputation. In a society where, until recently, major social differences were very limited, many a poor (and often blind) boy was able to leave his village, enrol in Al-Azhar and become a learned man. They come from all social classes and have followed all kinds of occupations. But there were other ranks, now less significant perhaps, that in different ways also brought prestige. Islam had many other aspects and various meanings.

Some families claim to be descendants of the prophet Mohammed. Such individuals or groups are called *ashraf* and, particularly in the past, often wore a green band round their turbans as a mark of status – however humble their lives might be. Whole villages sometimes prided themselves on their holy descent, or particular factions might produce genealogies backing their own claims and devaluing those of their rivals, another weapon in the arsenal of social competition. Many sheiks sought such a pedigree merely for the sake of

In 1920 Egypt was the first Muslim country to discard the veil; however it is still worn in the country and on government tourist posters.

social position. Then there are those who make the pilgrimage to the Holy Cities of Mecca and Medina and earn the title of Hajj, a mark of this highly meritorious act.

The only sizeable religious minority in Egypt are the Copts, a group which split off long ago from Greek Orthodoxy before the coming of the Arabs. Descendants of the ancient Egyptians, they were for a long time very much a separate community. Those who work the land often live in villages in which Copts are the majority of the population, though this is by no means always true. In the towns, the Copts tend to be concentrated in the same quarters. During the 19th century they were known for particular occupations, accountants and scribes, tradesmen, workers in precious metals, or builders and carpenters. In contemporary Egypt however, social distinctions between them and the rest of the population have largely disappeared. If a miracle is thought to have happened, whether in a church or a mosque, believers of both faiths will join in acclaiming it and will happily share local saints with no sense of sectarian division.

Predominant in the religious life of the mass of people were the saints and popular Sufism (mysticism). I vividly recall walking down a main Cairo street in the early hours of the morning some eight years ago. The city was utterly quiet. Then there rose and fell in the stillness a low murmur broken by pauses and choked weeping. Across the road was the tomb of a local saint – still triumphantly in his place amidst a cluster of new apartment blocks whose builders had wished to move his tomb but had had to bow to public pressure and leave him undisturbed. A man hung on to the grill of the small, square, domed building. He prayed for the saint's intercession, spoke entreatingly to him, and wept over a private misery that only the saint's assistance could mitigate. On another occasion, during a great pilgrimage to a saint's tomb in a market town, a peasant entered the crowded shrine room and after a brief prayer shouted at the saint as though to a friend across the street, and then went on to berate him soundly for failing to keep his part of a bargain made the previous year. So we should not be misled by the use of the word 'tombs'. The saints are, at least socially, very alive.

Every village has a shrine, and sometimes more than one, almost as marks of its separate identity. Leading rural families claim such a figure in their family. Urban quarters are guarded by the indefatigable care of these 'friends of God'. Stories of their ever continuing miracles are constant and never more so than on the great occasions of celebration of saints' days, the *mulids*.

Every village has its *mulid* and the towns have many. Some of the major festivals occur in succession and tradesmen, sweetsellers, tinkers and itinerant workers go on a circuit from town to town and saint to saint. These saints' days become minor pilgrimages. Families travel together and large groups go from the villages to camp for a day or two at a famous shrine. The most famous of them all, Seyyid Ahmad al-Bedawi of the delta market town of Tanta, is attended each year by almost a million people. Celebrations go on for a week and pilgrims pour in to visit him. The tiny room in the mosque where his tomb lies is packed with men, women and children. They circle his shrine, calling out, praying, weeping, wearing away the brass railing around it with pious hands seeking his *baraka* (blessing) through the touch of his shrine. Meanwhile mosque attendants stand on benches beating the crowd indiscriminately, urging it to keep moving. The chaos inside and outside has the atmosphere of a medieval fair. For the *mulids* are a time for trade and commerce, as well as for hymns and fireworks, sideshows and processions.

One of the five pillars of Islam is pilgrimage to Mecca. As a *fellah* sets out to the Holy City, the walls of his home are specially decorated.

These occasions were, until the first decades of the 20th century, dominated by groups known as the Sufi Orders. These were loosely organized associations of men joined together in obedience to a sheik who was thought to be descended by grace or family from the founding saint of the Order. For hundreds of years and in great profusion they were of vital importance in rural and urban Egypt, sometimes outweighing the influence of the orthodox Azhar. Prayers, hymns, books, meetings and education were often provided by their brotherhoods. It is not surprising that the Azharis at some periods were highly suspicious of the Sufis and all that they represented, though at others they were leading members

of the Orders.

Each brotherhood had its own banners, hymns and local centers. These were spread across the whole country in the case of famous groups like the *Shadhiliya* or *Ahmadiya* (followers of Ahmad al-Bedawi). Their sheiks emphasized particularly the links between individuals, God and the spiritual leaders. They performed, and still perform, rituals known as the *dhikr* made up of the rhythmic chanting of the names of God. Some groups were very austere in these performances, concentrating on chanting and the recitation of the Koran. Others, especially those made up of the mass of the poor, encouraged their adherents to escape from the routine miseries of everyday life into states of violent ecstasy and frenzied movement. Rituals that began with the slow chanting of 'Allah' and gentle movement back and forth would quickly build up into climaxes of explosive force as men staggered and jerked in religious intoxication. At one time some of the brotherhoods were famous for specific miracles, eating glass, handling snakes or self-mutilation without pain or scars.

The Sufi sheiks were often men of influence and power. But many had no formal religious training. Men usually belonged to several different orders at once, but nonetheless situations might arise in clan, village, town or province in which the leaders would compete with each other for followings and reputation. As ever, politics and religion were closely intertwined.

The saints remain as the sources of help and hope among the uncertainties of the world. But the brotherhoods and their sheiks have suffered a severe decline over the last 50 years. The rituals can still be seen, watched often by a crowd that looks on as much for entertainment or amusement as for religion. But the flags are seldom unfurled, local centers are shut down, and meetings are fewer and fewer. This decline is in part because of increasing opposition from the Azhari *ulema*. Since the late 19th century there has been a growing reformist movement in Islam, seeking some accommodation of the sweeping changes of our time, an up-dating of Muslim law and practice. Others have turned back to what they think of as a pure religion, uncontaminated by superstition or the worship of saints. By the 1930s, particularly in the rapidly expanding cities, new clubs, associations and organizations were set up, dedicated to the spread of literacy, sport, politics, education and economic cooperation. Popular Sufism no longer seems relevant to the needs of modern Egypt.

The parched and arid hills set aside for burial grounds contrast sharply with the vivid green of the narrow plain where the Nile flows.

In a village opposite Luxor on the Nile, a peasant family gathers after a hard day's work for a well deserved cup of coffee.

The *fellahin* find this storklike position very restful. This *fellah* stops to take a critical look at his newly tilled melon fields.

Politics and society have changed and left little room for the Sufi leaders to exercise their traditional role of mediation.

This, however, is far from saying that Egypt is a society in which religion has become unimportant. The bureaucracy and education may no longer be under the control of the *ulema* and sheiks whose place in social life, personal wealth and that of the mosques is much diminished. But the Azhar itself has benefitted from many reforms, and a greater intellectual and social vigor. Islam remains deeply embedded within the society. Men pray together, fast during the holy month of Ramadan, celebrate the two great festivals – one at the end of the fasting month, the other the feast of sacrifice. There is much visiting and gift-giving; they attend weddings and funerals and circumcisions held by friends, neighbors and family; they welcome pilgrims back from Arabia, go to *mulids* for the prophet and the saints.

Yet there are other, more subtle ways in which Islam is incorporated into the people's lives, into the values of the society and into a way of looking at the world. The Arabic word 'Islam' means submission, and the word usually translated as worshipper, *abd,* means servant or slave. This idea is dramatically pictured in the public prayers when the kneeling congregation bend forward, foreheads touching the ground, prostrating themselves in the direction of Mecca. This is perhaps *the* Muslim act, the perfect image of man's relation to God. Submission and contentment with what God

The staple food of most Egyptians is *pitta,* a round flat unleavened bread which is baked on the inside walls of a heated stone oven.

The methods of the *fellah* are as simple and ancient as his tools. If he needs extra water he will raise it himself or use the bull-drawn water wheel.

destines for man, acceptance and endurance, these are qualities that give so much of Egyptian life its simplicity, its emphasis on asceticism, its avoidance of display and its confidence. This often leads to a world-view that is somewhat sceptical, even pessimistic, and unwilling to accord the world too high a value in itself. *Ad-dunya zayy zift,* 'the world is rotten' (or literally, like pitch), is a characteristic Egyptian phrase, often said with a kind of wry amusement. Egyptians are famous throughout the middle east for their irrepressible joking on any subject under the sun, particularly concerning themselves and their rulers. This is often said to be a way of making centuries of oppression and alienation tolerable. They preserve that acute sense of the ridiculous which, for the poor or politically powerless, has always been the best weapon both of defense and of attack. The wide gulf that lies between appearance and reality, intention and action, promise and performance, is very clear to Egyptians and their biting wit and joking make much of it. Humor has become for them a way of saying very serious things about human nature and Egyptian history.

This is not to say that their attitudes do not have a very practical dimension. Egyptians are prepared for anything, able to account for anything, in a way that is not perhaps true of advanced industrial societies. Over the past fifty years or so many urban people have joined organizations based on religious foundations. They were dedicated to all kinds of things – literacy, leisure, discussion, economic improvement, reformism, nationalism, politics – and were one response to the often sweeping changes which have done so much to transform modern Egypt.

Just as the pyramids were the dead symbols of ancient Egypt, so the Aswan Dam is the living symbol of today's Egypt. Already most of the country's electricity is supplied by its huge turbines and thousands of acres of

People of Egypt

The temples of Ramses II and Nefertiti at Abu Simbel are threatened with flooding since the construction of Aswan dam. A rescue operation is now on.

Large quantities of water are needed to help the crops grow in Egypt's poor soil. In Nile-side villages it is fetched on muleback.

The construction of irrigation canals must precede any new inland settlement. In the new 'Province of the Liberation' a labor gang works hard.

desert land are being irrigated. But inevitably, with so huge and daring a scheme, problems have emerged too – water-borne liver parasites to cause disease, rising salinity of the soil, loss of the precious silt. Yet these problems pale beside the fact that the Nile has been harnessed. Nothing could be more fundamental in this river-made country. It marks, in part, the growth of Egypt's industrial sector, its working class and its need for energy; in part, the tremendous demand for more fertile land to provide for the exploding population; and in part to the way in which the whole country, this land of the peasant, is becoming more and more urban.

The actual part played by agriculture in the whole economy has shrunk. Fewer people work on the land; the land contributes less in terms of production. Many people have emigrated from the more densely crowded Upper Egypt to Lower Egypt and the delta. Others have simply left the country altogether for the towns.

No city has grown more than Cairo. In 1917 this was a town of 791,000 people. By 1937 it had reached 1,312,000 and twenty years later 2,091,000. By 1973 it was probably something over 6 million. As a capital it dominates the rest of the country more than it should, and not only in size. Communications, culture, industry, services, construction, government and the enormous bureaucracy, all are controlled from Cairo. The city as a result attracts to itself more people than it can reasonably accommodate. So the traffic between town and country is very much a two-way affair. In 1960, for example, about 40 per cent of Cairo's population was from outside. In a sense, therefore, if the capital has absorbed the countryside, the reverse has also occurred, and the peasantry has taken over much of the urban area. Each area has its own characteristics, its own arrangement of space and pattern of life. Wandering round some of the outer parts, you almost return to village life. Here, once again, is the world of the *fellahin* in dress, speech and habit. The houses are the same mud brick – a village in the town. And indeed the immigrants often cluster together in groups of relatives and neighbors from the same quarter, the same village or region. They are still as poor as peasants too, living at the same low subsistence level and often still illiterate. The men can only expect semi-skilled work at the best and their women eleven or twelve children, of whom six or seven will probably survive.

Other quarters, deeper in the city, have staggering densities of up to 100,000 people to the square kilometer. though the people have lived there longer. In yet another part thousands live in the grimly named 'cities of the dead'. These are old cemeteries in which squatters have settled over the years, first in the tombs and then later built their own houses. This peculiar slum area has become a part of the living Cairo – despite all the difficulties of providing sewage, drainage and education.

Egyptians are a highly sophisticated people with a long cultural tradition. Illiteracy is no bar to the famous sense of humor, the capacity for wit, word-play and repartee. Crowds in the cinema or at the theater are more participants than audience, shouting out usually unprintable comments to the film stars and keeping up a run of ironic or blunt commentaries which are far more entertaining than the film itself. A celebrated singer's concert will be heard all over the country on blaring radios in cafés, garages, houses, shops and factories. The listeners sway entranced, click their fingers, eyes half closed, and slide into a dream-like ecstasy over the long, swooning loops of the voice. *Keif,* delight, an absolute pleasure; how often the word is used! The echoing smack of the draughts as men play backgammon in a coffee shop. Then hours of talk and slowly sipped cups of coffee or terrifyingly strong black tea, long evenings with a pack of cards and a singer's voice and uproarious humor; the elaborate courtesies of visiting and hospitality; the lights and chanting of a celebration for the prophet, a procession for the new year; avidly watched football matches and violent partisanship; a feeling, despite all that this dubious world can do, of a certain character, a certain confidence, a certain feeling of being Egyptian.

The striking face of this Egyptian peasant woman is unveiled, but she wears a black veil on her head to indicate that she is married.

Teda
Chad

Only a few Teda remain in the village all year with the slaves and serfs. The rest of the families return with their herds for the date harvest.

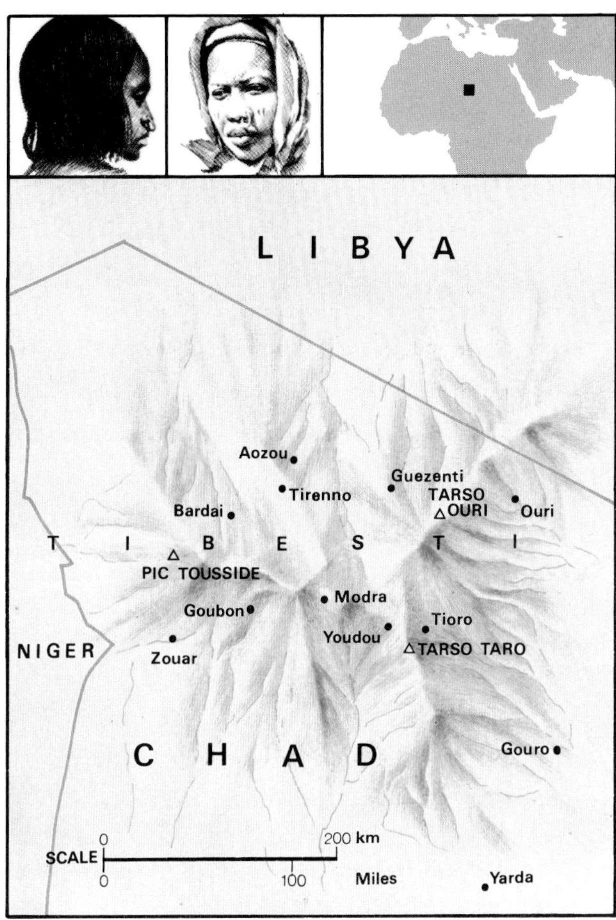

The Sahara is a vast and arid desert, unfriendly to human life. Within an area almost as great as that of the United States and greater than that of Europe, the Sahara supports a population of no more than 2·5 million people. The history of these people has been governed by the nature of the environment – and also by the fact that they now live at the end of a long process of ecological contraction. For the Sahara was once a fertile place, with lakes and rivers that were fished extensively. Climatic changes which reduced it to a desert may have been helped along by imprudent farming which, elsewhere, has produced dust-bowls. However, over the past 2,000 years, the steady decrease in rainfall and the gradual impoverishment of the land have subjected the people to factors which have not permitted most of them to develop a settled life. Many of these people are nomads herding camels and donkeys, sheep and goats over vast areas, moving constantly to find new pasture as soon as the old grazing lands are exhausted. The 10,000 Teda, or Tibu, are among these nomadic peoples, living on the Tibesti *massif* which lies in the south-eastern part of the central Sahara in Chad.

The Teda are a poor people who have nonetheless

established a working relationship with the desert. In contrast with other nomadic peoples of the Sahara who are Berber or Arab, they are more or less negroid in appearance, with dark hair and skins; apart from certain Berber elements in their speech – probably picked up from their Tuareg neighbors – their language is of unknown origin. The partially Islamic customs of the Teda are accompanied by certain older pagan customs – for example oaths are sworn on the Koran, but with the very un-Muslim understanding that anyone who swears a false oath will die within a year. This ambiguity is particularly apparent in the woman's status. She has little to say in the choice of her husband; she may never eat in his presence; her blood-price is only half of his. But a Teda woman does have other rights and within the home they override those of the men. If a husband challenges his wife's authority at home, she may beat him.

If a husband is rash enough to insult his wife in public, a set ritual retaliation is open to her – if sufficiently goaded, she will strip herself naked before all present and then retreat in offended dignity to her hut. Often Teda women are formidable and where they once wore swords they now carry daggers. The occasional pitched battle between women are affairs in which the men dare not interfere. Overall, however, it is the men who dominate Teda society. Rank and property are inherited through the male line; a father has greater authority and commands greater respect from his children.

A Teda boy comes of age when he is circumcised at about the age of 12 or 14. The young boys are circumcised in groups at the time of the date harvest by old men of the *haratin* class who are deemed to have certain magical qualities. On these occasions there are goat sacrifices and lavish feasts which often end as drunken and violent orgies. Yet among the Teda families and clans there is much cooperation and aid at times of need, extending even to active support in blood-feuds. Murder is no rare thing and, when committed in the course of a feud, it does not bring social condemnation upon the murderer. Nevertheless a killer will take ritual precautions – he will change his name; to deter his pursuers, he may sacrifice a goat and hobble himself with the animals' intestines, then upon breaking free of these, he magically releases himself from danger. A blood-feud can continue indefinitely, with revenge killings and counter killings until stopped by the payment of a blood-price – which is often prohibitively large.

The Teda, under the nominal authority of a single chief or *dardai,* are divided into some 40 clans which range from a few 'noble' clans (said to be descendants of the first conquerors of the Tibesti) to the negro slaves. But they are now no longer desert raiders, nor slavers, and now trading is mainly concerned with things like dates and salt, goats and millet. And the Teda caravans carrying noble tribesmen dressed in magical skins become more and more a memory of the past.

Teda women are as fierce as the men. If a husband grossly insults his wife in public she is likely to strip off her clothes and walk away.

Rock engravings and paintings are found throughout the Sahara. These engravings show cattle with distinctly marked coats and distorted horns.

(Top) The women love elaborate silver jewelry which is made locally. Most of them wear a silver nose ring in the form of a snake.

Murder and lengthy blood-feuds involving whole clans are not unusual among the Teda. A murderer performs elaborate rituals against capture.

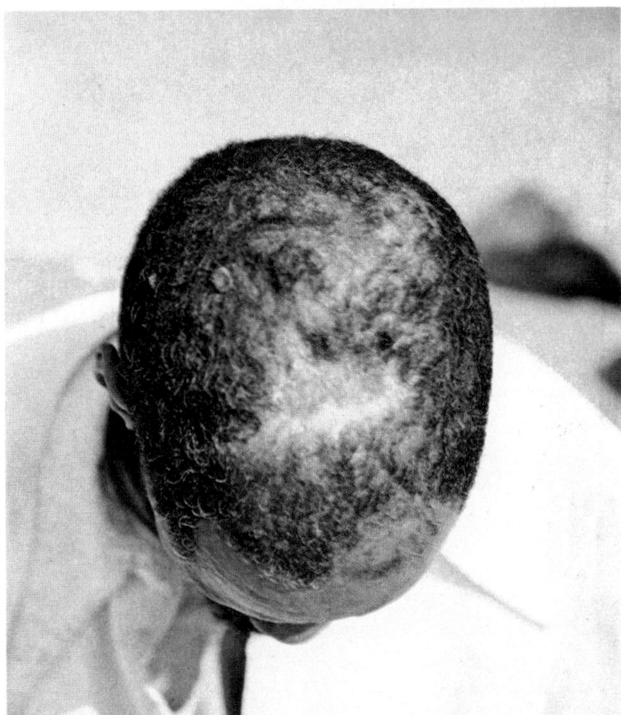

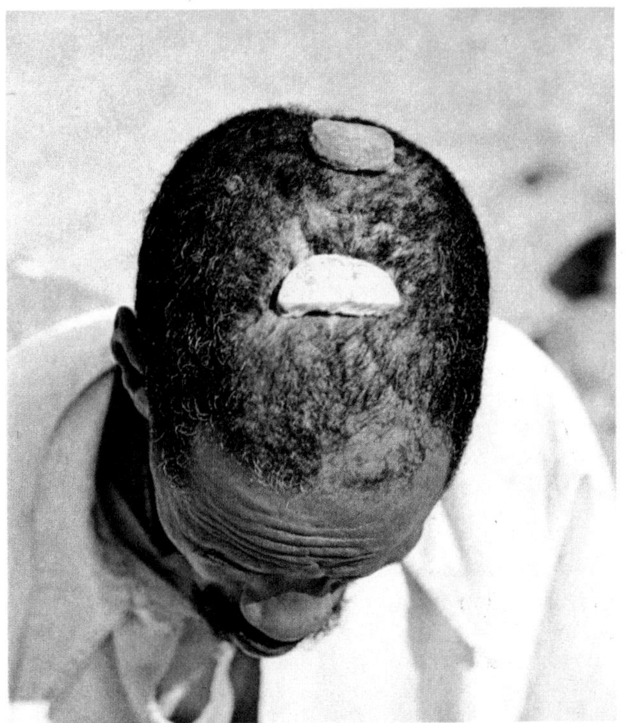

Trepanning, removal of a small piece of skull-bone, is done to cure headaches and to let evil spirits escape from inside the head.

(Top) The local 'doctor' uses an old pen-knife, a 6-inch nail and some metal probes. The patient must be held down as there is no anaesthetic.

After the operation the bone fragments are placed on top of the scars. They are lucky charms and will prevent the headaches recurring.

Druzes
Lebanon, Syria and Israel

The Druzes are one of the most elusive and mysterious of the middle east's religious sects. Isolated by generations of mountain life and shunning all strangers, secrecy is the strictest injunction of their faith. It has made them self-reliant, semi-nationalistic and distinctive in looks as well as beliefs. They have lived in the Levant since ancient times and there are now about 200,000 in Syria, 70,000 in Lebanon, and in Israel about 33,000, double the number there in 1948.

The Druzes are stocky people. Their faces are broad and short, often pale-skinned, gray-eyed, handsome and firm of chin. Druze women, especially the fair ones, are considered beautiful. Such is their physical distinctiveness that there have been many rumors of their origins. Early travelers noticed their fairness and thought they must be Europeans. Others wrote that they must be a lost tribe of Israel, fled from the wrath of Moses when he smashed the Golden Calf. The most persistent tale was that they were a remnant of the Crusaders, followers of the Comte de Dreux, who had marched his men into the mountains after the fall of Acre.

Druze religion originated in Cairo in the 10th century. It was born of Islam, yet the Druzes are not really Muslims at all. They renounce the prophet, the Koran and all the rules of Islam. They emerged from the Shi'ite branch of Islam. The Shi'ites, unlike Sunni Muslims, believe that their imams are descended from Ali, the prophet's son-in-law and are endowed with divine power. The Ismaelis are a branch of the Shi'ites and the Druzes splintered away from the Ismaelis. The name Druze owes its birth to Al-Darazi – meaning 'tailor' in Persian – who was at the Cairo court of Al-Hakim, the sixth, and according to the Druzes, the last imam. Al-Darazi preached that Al-Hakim should be venerated as the true God.

Al-Hakim was an extraordinary character. His mother was Christian, but he sacked the Church of the Holy Sepulchre in Jerusalem, adding tension to the already sticky relations between Christians and Muslims. In fact he desecrated Christian shrines throughout his realm and his acts led ultimately to the Crusades. He killed all the dogs in Cairo because one barked at him, but, to those who venerated him, his eccentricities were taken as a sign of his superhumanness.

Finding no response to his new creed among the Egyptians Al-Darazi migrated to the foot of Mount Hermon in Lebanon. Here his faith was cradled. It flowered among the mountain people there. In Lebanon, the home of many creeds, one may still find a cedar over two thousand years old, outdating Christianity, Islam and Druzism. In this land of green valleys, where cypresses, pines and olives grow in abundance on the mountain slopes and flowers tremble on the valley floors was the first home of the Druzes. Later they spread into the Shuf district east of Beirut where the Crusaders found them and where many still flourish. From Shuf some migrated in the early 18th century to Hawran over the border in Syria.

Druzism has been cloaked in mystery and speculation for centuries. A Christian traveler, Benjamin of Tudela, came across them in 1170 beneath the slopes of Mount Hermon and wrote: 'They are called heathen and unbelievers, because they confess to no religion. Their dwellings are on the summits of mountains and in the ridges of rocks, and they are subject to no king or prince . . . This people live incestuously; a father cohabits with his own daughter, and once every year all men and women assemble to celebrate a festival, upon which occasion, after eating and drinking they hold promiscuous intercourse . . .'

It may possibly be true that at the very beginning of their history the Druzes did allow a certain amount of sexual license to increase their numbers, but not for long and since then they have been monogamous. In other respects the description is misleading. The Druzes preach a simple creed of love and truth. They concentrate on lifting up their hearts to God. Most of their theology was formed by Hamzah, the successor to Al-Darazi. He

Only at 40 is it possible for a Druze, like this shepherd, to receive full initiation into the Middle East's most secretive sect.

completely severed the tie with Islam. He eliminated all ritual from his theology. He ordered that all old faiths must be renounced, and all those who 'live in error' – non-Druzes – must be kept away. He recognized the divine principle in humanity, adhered fully to his lord – Al-Hakim – and claimed absolute resolution to his will. Others through him should do likewise. It was through the teaching and influence of Hamzah that the Druzes really became established as a united religious community.

But why did this worship of an eccentric in Cairo many miles away take hold in Lebanon? The answer, or part of it, is probably that the people were Ismaeli Shi'ites, and so already believed in the principle of divine humanity. They were poor peasants into the bargain, and ridden with hardships. Moreover the promised Mahdi, who was to restore a better world, had not yet come and there was a general feeling of frustration. They were receptive to new teaching. To the surrounding Sunni Muslims and the Shi'ites they were heretics. Hence the Druzes did not publicly disclaim Islam, but surrounded their religion in vaguenesses. The sacred books handed down by Hamzah, all handwritten as they are to this day, became the secret books and the Druzes withdrew into themselves.

The door has been closed to those wishing to enter or leave the Druzes since that first generation of proselytizers. But there have been exceptions, such as the admittance of a few wealthy Arab families who are still the aristocracy of Druze society.

Not all Druzes are acquainted with the sacred books. There are two kinds of Druzes: the Knowledgeable Ones and the Ignorant. One in seven is a Knowledgeable One. He abstains from drinking and smoking, refrains from abusive language, shuns unlawful gain and conducts himself with the utmost decorum and uprightness. He is outwardly distinguished by his heavy white turban and huge white untrimmed beard, for he must be over 40 to be a Knowledgeable One.

Every Thursday there are meetings in inconspicuous little rooms on the hill tops. In subdued light one sees divans around the walls and the tomb of a holy man in the center. Here is where the sacred books are read, still in their handwritten form. If a stranger comes, the Druzes will not throw him out. On the contrary they will invite him to their meeting and politely read a text from the Koran for him if he is Muslim, or a text from the Bible if he is Christian. Only when the stranger has gone will they bring out their sacred books and continue to read their secret scriptures.

The Ignorant Druzes are only half learned in the religion of their society, for they cannot go to the weekly meetings to hear the sacred scriptures. They live much as the surrounding Arabs do, in little mountain villages, tending their goats, or growing fruit in their orchards, picking olives from their groves. Their houses have tall rooms with tiled floors to keep them cool. The women move silently in the background, never intruding upon the men but cooking for them and serving them with the patience of slaves.

In Israel the Druzes are well off compared to their fellows in Syria and Lebanon. In 1957 the Israeli government recognized the Druzes' right to jurisdiction in matters of personal status. In turn they support the Israeli government, for in the words of one old patriarch of 94: 'In my opinion, whoever lets you live, and is in power, should get your support.' The Druzes in Israel live in 17 villages all in Galilee except for two near the foot of Mount Carmel. Nine of these villages, high in the mountains, where they have stood for centuries, are entirely Druze. The other seven are mixed Druze and Christian-Arab. In 1948, at the end of the British Mandate, no village had running water or electricity. Only a few could be reached by car and 95 per cent of the population was illiterate. Now all villages have running water, most have electricity and each one has an elementary school where boys get compulsory education and 80 per cent of the girls are taught.

The family traditions have changed too. No longer is the father-herdsman the breadwinner, but the son who has gone to work in the docks and factories of Haifa and Eilat. In Eilat a permanent Druze settlement is being built. There is compulsory military service for men but not for women, unlike the Israelis. Most serve as border guards and are reputed for their ferocity. In the mountain villages light textile factories have been built where the women can earn a little extra money. A significant number of young Druzes have begun to go to university. There are one or two Druzes in political and governmental positions, and the number of educated Druzes is increasing all the time.

In Lebanon some of the young Druzes have relinquished their beliefs and have become completely assimilated into Lebanese society. This could not happen in Israel, since however well they are tolerated there the Druzes could never become assimilated into Jewish society. In the older history of the Lebanon the Druzes kept very much to themselves as many do today. Yet, in certain regions, they wielded considerable power and leadership.

It is not long since 1860 when they attacked a group of Maronite Christians and pursued the fugitives to Seraglio where they had sought the protection of the Turks. The Druzes were backed by the Turks and although the Maronites were locked into a courtyard the Druzes climbed over the walls and continued the slaughter. In 1949 the courtyard was excavated and 15 sackfuls of bones were removed and enshrined. Some Christians in Lebanon still feel bitter. But the Druzes have always had influence and power disproportionate to their numbers, largely because of the discipline of their religion and their code of always looking after their brothers. They have always had to fight to keep their identity and to be allowed to practise their own distinctive religion.

Tunisian villagers
Tunisia

In a country where only one crop every 7 years may survive drought, villagers say stoically 'Between sweetness and bitterness our lives are spent.'

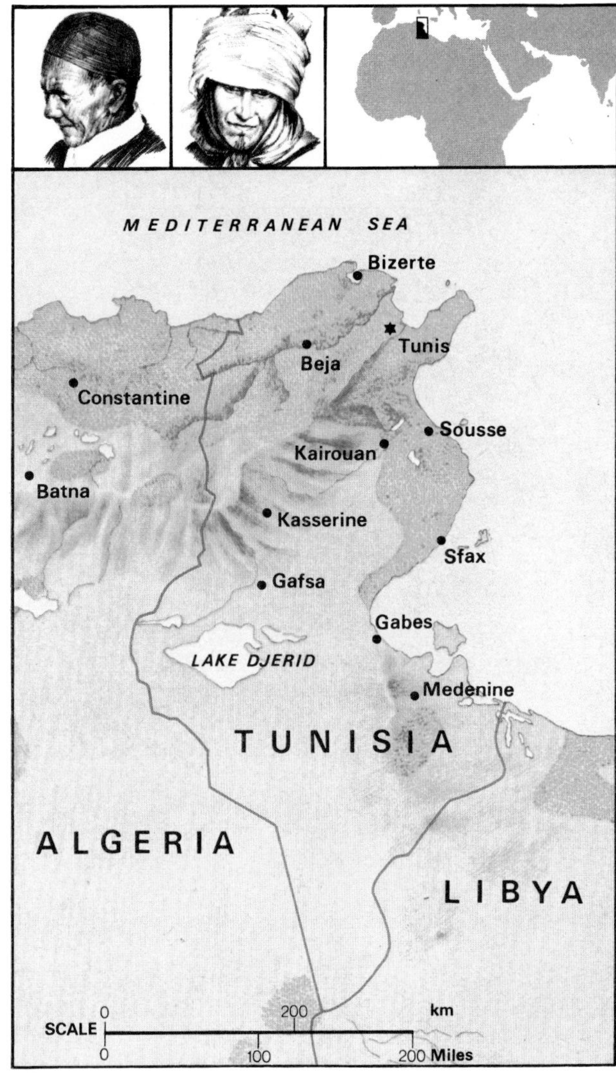

Days of plenty are rare in Tunisian villages. Droughts and floods may ruin villagers' crops and animals. In the Sahel province, where the land is unirrigated, the rain is so irregular that villagers have a good crop in only one of every seven years. In that year they store as much as they can to use in the poor years.

Farming has been the basis of village life for centuries. Land is plowed in spring and autumn and crops are harvested in mid-November. Men do the heavy work like drawing water from the wells, plowing the land or climbing into the trees to pick olives. Women do easier work like picking up olives which have fallen to the ground, looking after the animals or raising chickens. At home they have more to do. Besides looking after children they cook meals, bake bread and clean the house. They also spin wool to sell in the weekly markets or weave it at home to make the material for men's clothes and women's winter shawls. They may weave blankets either to sell, or for a bride's trousseau.

Homes in Natmata on the edge of the Sahara are burrowed out of the rock itself. Ventilation shafts are sunk to let in air and light.

In some villages women specialize in rug weaving. Each region has its own designs and special material of either cotton or wool. The government encourages rug weaving to try and diversify village economy. It buys and sells the products and organizes rug exhibitions, and centers where women can learn to weave free of charge. Some women make dresses and embroider bridal linen to sell to the townspeople. Some make clay kitchen utensils, again for sale in the towns.

Since independence in 1956 women have been encouraged to continue their education and to work in towns. Some village women now work as primary school teachers. One finds them working as sales assistants in big department stores in the nearby cities or as midwives or nurses at hospitals there. One often sees a woman riding behind her husband on his motorcycle, both of them on their way to work in the city. Many women are telephonists and receptionists in tourist hotels.

Children go to school in the morning and afternoon. Schools are crowded and there are neither enough classrooms nor enough teachers: classrooms are used in shifts. After school boys go to play in the street or run errands for their mothers while girls help their mothers with the household chores.

Evenings are a precious time for the family. They are by themselves and the village is quiet save for the occasional barking of a dog or the noise of a camel. In summer, when it is cool and pleasant after a hot day, the family eat their meal in the courtyard, under a grape vine or a pomegranate tree. They spend the rest of the evening listening to the radio, drinking tea and nibbling nuts. If they can afford it they will have chopped almonds or peanuts in their tea as well. In summer they also may go to a family wedding party or a circumcision ceremony. Nobody calls on a family in the evenings except a brother or a brother's son or another close relative. In winter they eat their evening meal in the room where they all sleep, and sit together on one bed with a single blanket to warm the whole family. They make tea on the *kanum* – a clay container where all food is cooked – or over burning charcoal, warming the room at the same time.

The founder of a Tunisian village is usually a saint. He is believed to be endowed with some of the grace of God – *baraka*. He can therefore help others during his life-time and after his death. He can only help people if they visit the shrine where he is buried, read the first chapter of the Koran to him, bring him candles or incense or a beautiful piece of material to hang over his tomb, or do all of these things. The saints' descendants are believed to inherit some of his *baraka* and they too can help people. The shrine of a saint is the focal point of community life. It is usually in the center of a complex of buildings which include a mosque where people pray their five daily prayers, a small Koranic school for children to learn the Koran by heart, several rooms for visitors who wish to stay overnight, kitchens where they can cook their food, and bathrooms. There is a large courtyard too, where both villagers and visitors celebrate

Rock houses stay cool but they are dank, dark and smelly. Most people enter by the door. Ropes are only for the agile.

On the island of Djerba, off the Tunisian coast, young girls draw water from a deep well. Even though it is deep, water must be used sparingly.

(Bottom) Each house has a *kanum*, clay oven, in the courtyard. Flat unleavened bread is baked against the side of the oven.

the annual festival of the village's patron saint.

Important religious ceremonies take place in the shrine under the protection of the saint. Circumcisions are performed while relatives sing and dance in the courtyard. Before marriage a girl will visit the shrine with her friends and later her betrothed for the saint's blessing.

Each patron saint has his own particular personal characteristics. One saint will be renowned for his strictness, and visitors to his shrine have to be careful not to offend him. Another may be very patient with his visitors. A third will be renowned for his love of wealth and a fourth for his passion for fame. The shrine of Sidi Bu-Rawi in the city of Sousse is endowed with large estates but the shrine of Sidi Ameur who is the founder of a village in the Sahel province which is named after him, is not wealthy but famous. It is said that when the treasures of the world were opened up for them, Sidi Bu-Rawi asked for wealth and Sidi Ameur demanded fame and the ability of his descendants to write charms for whose efficacy he would be responsible.

As well as these personal characteristics each saint is believed to excel in a particular ritual ability. It is usually the power to heal a particular ailment. One saint, for

Escorted by musicians, a young bride goes to her new home. Before the wedding she and her betrothed will have asked blessing from the village saint.

Dates are one of the few crops that grow in the dry south. Quantities are picked every year for sale abroad as well as for home consumption.

example, might be especially good at healing people suffering from jaundice, a second in healing people suffering from skin ailments. A third may help women who have difficulties in childbirth. A fourth may exorcise *jinn* or harmful spirits from those possessed by them.

In every village the anniversary of the patron saint is a feast day. People from many different towns and villages will come to partake in the saint's *baraka* – godly grace – and to be healed if they are suffering from the complaints in which he specializes. Villagers take advantage of the occasion to sell their local crafts.

The saint's shrine is built in the most attractive part of the village: on the sea shore if it is a coastal one, or on the highest spot overlooking the sea if it is inland. Families may travel a long way with their blankets, stoves and food for this pilgrimage-cum-holiday. They also bring a 'promised gift' for the saint which may be a lamb, a chicken or a goat. They bring drums and their tambourines, and if the village is on the shore, their swimming costumes. They swim, cook, eat, gossip, sing and dance as well as reading the first chapter of the Koran to the saint and invoking him to protect them and guard the health of their children. They sing religious hymns in praise of the prophet Mohammed and the saint whose anniversary they are celebrating.

The most respected people in a Tunisian village are the descendants of the village's founder and patron saint. They represent the highest stratum of village life. They receive the gifts given to him by visitors, and have all the guests to look after. They write charms for them and heal them through the *baraka* they have inherited from their saintly forefather.

Villagers are strongly attached to their ancestors. They inherit from them their village land, their names, their

The bride is decked out in all the family heirlooms. Before the ceremony village women gather for a party at her house.

Lambs horns are used to strip olives from their branches. In some parts of the country this is men's work only.

distinguishing customs and conventions which they call the 'innermost values of the community'. The saintly founder of the village is the figure around whom history and traditions revolve.

Two of the most important feasts are the Muslim feasts of *'id al-Fitr* at the end of the month of fasting, Ramadan, and *'id al-Adha*. This commemorates the time when, according to Iṣlam, Abraham sacrificed a lamb instead of his son Isma'il, the ancestor of the Arabs. These two feasts start with prayers at dawn in the village mosque, followed by a long procession to the shrine of the patron saint of the village. They sing religious hymns and when they reach the shrine they read the first chapter of the Koran. Then they visit the tomb of their dead where they again read the first chapter of the Koran. Only then can men join their wives and children for breakfast and begin making merry. They eat lots of pastries and sweets and drink mint tea. Children receive money, gifts and new clothes from the grand-parents, parents, uncles and aunts.

Family connections are strong. All the inhabitants of a village quarter are the descendants of one ancestor, or so they claim. All families are at some point connected by marriage. Tunisians value highly these ties of kinship and marriage. Above all they value their ancestors and their parents. If a man wants to thank a person for rendering him a service and show the utmost respect he would say to his benefactor 'May God have mercy on your parents'. He means ancestors as well.

Tunisians hate to leave their birthplace. If they have to work in another town they do not live there but ride miles back at the end of the day on their bicycles, motor-cycles, cars or buses. People are surprised if a person leaves his place of origin and moves to live in another village. They usually think he has disgraced himself for why else would he leave his home and family and live where nobody knows him, where he has no connections and where he is ignorant of the innermost values of the community? They have little respect for outsiders.

These values, in which the family is held in such importance, conflict with harsh economic conditions caused by the droughts and floods as well as the fact that the land cannot support the increasing population. Better medical care has decreased the rate of infant mortality, but in spite of the government encouragement to diversify their economy some Tunisians are forced to leave their villages and emigrate to France, West Germany and Libya. They always try to return for holidays bringing with them the latest European fashions. They come back to fulfill the vows they may have made to the patron saint of their village. As custom demands they do this by slaughtering an animal and inviting the villagers to participate in a feast for the saint. They then sing the usual mystic hymns in praise of the prophet and the saint; reflecting on the events of their life they say 'Between sweetness and bitterness our lives are spent'.

Tuareg
Sahara desert

Tuareg men veil themselves while their beautiful women do not. This girl in Abalak, Niger Republic, is made-up for the Independence Day celebration.

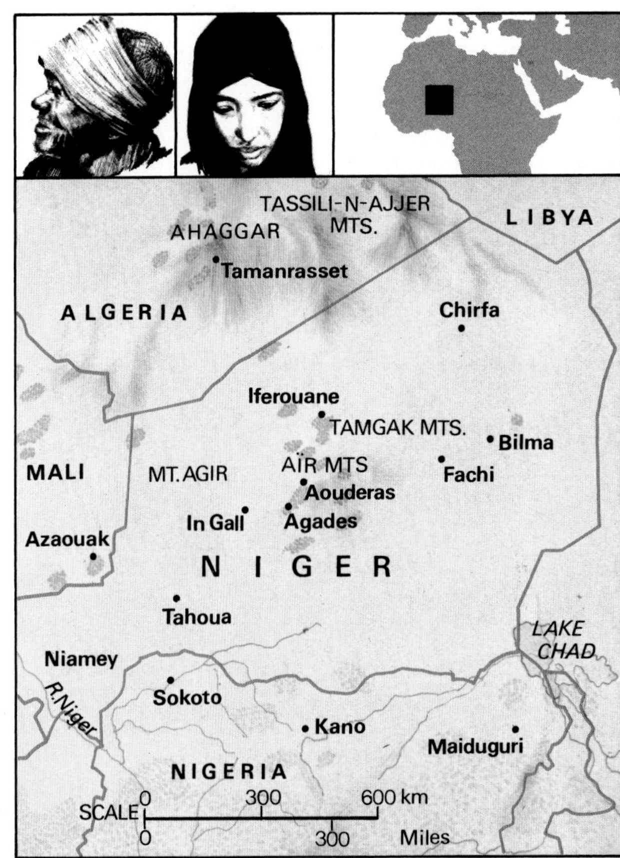

Far away to the south of Algeria, in the trackless wastes of the Sahara, there lives a race of marauding nomads, who, on account of their impious character, have been named by the Arabs 'Tawarek' or 'God-forsaken'.

This opening to a book by an Englishman in North Africa in 1903 is typical of the extensive romantic literature on the Tuareg, which was nourished by the Tuareg's inaccessibility and their habit of killing early European travelers. The Tuareg were said to be mysterious and cruel, of Christian (possibly Crusader) origin, and seven feet tall. They are white Berbers, descendants of the early inhabitants of northern Africa. The Arab invasions of the 7th and 11th centuries submerged the Berber tribes from Libya to Mauritania, but the Tuareg remained masters of the Sahara and kept the Arabs out. There are records of veiled Berbers, who must be Tuareg, in the chronicles of Arab travelers from the 10th century onwards. By the 15th century the Tuareg were trading with the Portuguese in west Africa, and they controlled the trans-Sahara caravans which carried slaves, ivory, gold, ostrich and lion skins to the Mediterranean and middle east. In the south, the Tuareg occupied Timbuctu on a number of occasions and dominated the middle course of the Niger.

The 19th-century European exploration of the Sahara first brought the Tuareg to general notice, and from the

An early traveler reported that there lived in the trackless wastes of the Sahara a race of marauding nomads, called Tawarek, or 'God forsaken', by the Arabs.

1850s the French began to occupy central Algeria. The Tuareg wiped out the expeditionary force of Colonel Flatters in 1881, but were unable to resist the heavily armed Foureau-Lamy mission which crossed the Sahara in 1898-99. The Ahaggar Tuareg were defeated by the French at the battle of Tit in 1902 and in the following years most of the Saharan Tuareg submitted uneasily to French administration.

Now there are probably 3 to 400,000 Tuareg occupying a million square miles of the Sahara (an area equivalent to all of western Europe including the United Kingdom), divided politically among the republics of Algeria, Libya, Niger and Mali.

The Tuareg live in a variety of landscapes in the Sahara and the belt of dry steppe vegetation along its southern edge. Almost everywhere it is a difficult life. In summer temperatures of 50°C (122°F) in the shade are not rare, while sand and rock exposed to the sun can reach 75° or 80°C (175°F). Rain is erratic and in some places several years may pass between showers. High winds and sandstorms are common. Some nomad groups live in the central Saharan mountain ranges.

The Ajjer Tuareg inhabit the Tassili n Ajjer, a crumbling black mountain range on the frontier between Algeria and Libya. The soft sandstone of the Tassili has been cut by torrents in the past into deep canyons and valleys, and wind erosion continues to sculpt the rock of the plateau into strange aerodynamic shapes. At some early period, when the Sahara was less hostile, several Mediterranean plants crossed the thousand miles of steppe and colonized the Tassili; when the desert dried up again relics of this vegetation were left behind, and have continued to reproduce, so that the Tassili has oleanders, olives, figs and giant cypresses among the more conventional desert thorn trees.

To the west the higher mountain massif of the Ahaggar is occupied by the Kel Ahaggar Tuareg. A mass of jagged black peaks and lava plains, the Ahaggar is the backbone of the Sahara and rises in places to 9,000 feet. Like the Tassili, its vegetation contains Mediterranean relics, but plants of any sort are rare and concentrated into a few wadis, or dried river beds where, after a storm, water runs again for a few hours. Kel Ahaggar tents are pitched beside the wadis, and their goats feed on the thorn trees but there is not enough pasture here in the mountains for camels, which are kept in the Tamesna plains to the south. The Kel Ahaggar, like the Kel Ajjer, own date palms and gardens in the oases, but the work is mostly done by sedentary black Haratin and slaves.

South of the Ahaggar are two smaller mountain ranges, the Aïr and the Adrar n Iforas, each inhabited by Tuareg. The plants and animals here are more closely related to those of tropical Africa, and there is more rain. Further south still, Tuareg live in the very dry savanna belt on both banks of the Niger, from the Timbuctu and the Niger bend, east through the territory of the Iwllemmeden almost to Lake Chad. Rain and richer pasture enables these southern Tuareg to keep cattle as well as camels, sheep and goats, and here the nomadism of the central Saharan Tuareg becomes a much less extensive and more seasonal transhumance.

Tuareg are tall (though not seven feet) and slim as befits a desert people. They dress against the heat in ample, loose clothes: the men wear baggy trousers of blue or black cotton, held up by a decorated leather drawstring, a loose white cotton shirt, a flowing ankle-length black or blue *gandoura* or Arab robe. In the mountains of the north, where frosts are common, the men wear black and brown striped woolen kashabirs, and a huge camel hair burnous, or hooded cloak, on cold desert nights. The women dress uniformly in a black shift, with a length of the same cloth over their head, held in place with a counterweight, usually the large decorated key to their camel bag, hanging over their shoulder. Men and women wear leather sandals, often highly decorated, and a few verses of the Koran enclosed in small leather pouches as charms around their necks or arms. The women make up their eyes with antimony, and occasionally decorate their faces with a brown ochre

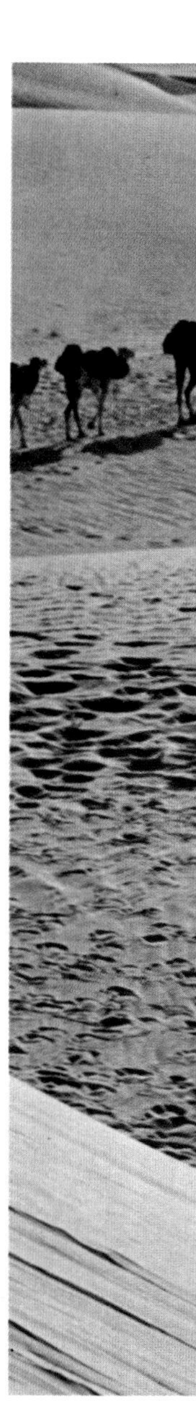

Returning to their camp in the Aïr mountains from the salt pans at Bilma a laden caravan crosses the waterless Tenere desert.

Women share a pot of tea. Hitched onto the left of the tent are two leather bags in which husband and wife keep their clothing.

Years of drought and uncertain rainfall make every trek a risk for the Tuareg. They do not always find the *guelta*, rock pool, containing water.

With a hot iron a man burns a blister caused by the heavy salt packs from his camel's flank. A young slave holds the camel's head.

A girl pulls a baby camel back to its stake after it has finished suckling. Tuareg women have more freedom than other Muslim women.

(Right) Men swathe themselves in a 15-foot veil as protection against sun, sand and wind. Complex rules govern adjustment of the veil before strangers.

powder. Their hair is tightly combed from a central parting into plaits on either side, and they wear bead and leather bracelets. They are often very beautiful.

The most striking item of Tuareg dress, and the root of their mysterious reputation, is the veil worn by all adult men. The veil is a five yard strip of black or white cloth, wrapped around the head and neck leaving only a narrow slit for the eyes. On important occasions rich Tuareg wear a veil of indigo blue cloth, which shines in the sunlight with a purplish metallic sheen. The indigo dye easily rubs off onto the skin, giving the men's faces and beards a bluish tinge which is much admired, particularly since the high price of indigo cloth makes it a visible sign of wealth. Rich women may also wear an indigo shawl instead of the usual black one and they often rub the cloth against their faces to accentuate the blue sheen of their skin. The men's veil almost certainly has a utilitarian origin – anyone who travels in the Sahara in the hot season quickly finds out that some protection against the heat and dryness of the air is essential, and a veil, like a deep-sea diver's helmet, keeps the air around the wearer's face breathable. But the veil has also come to have ritual significance. The higher the social position of the wearer, the more particular he is likely to be; Tuareg meeting important strangers hitch their veil so high that their eyes are almost hidden, and then drink their tea under the veil so as not to reveal their mouths. However, the days of great veil etiquette seem to be passing and around the camp with people they know, many Tuareg are no longer so particular, and some will even remove and retie their veil in a stranger's presence.

Tuareg men all carry knives, and some still wear swords – long, straight-bladed weapons with decorated leather hilts and scabbards. Men used to carry shields of decorated oryx antelope skin, but these have now disappeared, with the increasing rarity of the oryx. In winter camps, when there is little to do, the Tuareg fence with their swords and knives, and swords are still used in occasional fights over the right to draw water at disputed wells.

The Tuareg produce little art, but practical leather objects made by women and blacksmiths are usually highly decorated. All women are adept at working and dyeing leather, and bags, whips, saddles and harnesses, sheaths, scabbards and tobacco pouches are decorated in basic colors – red, yellow, pale green and black – with sharp geometric shapes. The blacksmiths work iron, brass and wood, and although some of the older sword blades came from Spain or Germany, Tuareg smiths are enormously resourceful: sword and knife blades are now made from lorry springs, their hilts from landrover body panels and bakelite battery casings, while brass and copper are taken from cartridge cases and electrical wire. Camel saddles have a small seat with a high back and a large pommel in the form of a cross, richly decorated in metal and colored leather. The rider crosses his legs and rests his bare feet on the camel's back, pushing rhythmically at the speed he wishes the animal to move; the camel is guided by a single rein attached to its nostril.

Tents are made from sheep and goat skins, tanned and dyed with dark red clay, then sewn together; 30 or 40 skins will make a normal tent, but up to 60 or 70 are needed for the tent of an important chief. The skins are supported on wooden tent poles, the central ones being carved with geometric patterns and hatchings. Most tents have side walls of grass matting, decorated with colored leather thongs. Some of the southern Tuareg live in tents made from straw or from palm leaves arranged over semi-circular wooden frames.

All Tuareg speak the same language, Tamashek or Tamahak, and although they have no written literature, and almost nothing to write with or on, there is a written alphabet called *tifinar* which is related to the ancient Phoenician script. Many Tuareg can read *tifinar,* but its future is uncertain since the only formal education any Tuareg children receive is in either Arabic or French. The older people see *tifinar* as part of the Tuareg culture which will probably disappear.

Women play a single-cord violin, the *imzad,* the sound box of which is made by stretching a skin across an

A woman prepares millet in an earthenware jar resting on the embers. She will eat with the children after the men have been served.

enamel bowl. A drum is similarly made by stretching a wet skin across a grain mortar, and men sometimes play a wooden flute. Parties are held around camp fires in the evening and both men and women sing. On such occasions the children tell animal fables: 'Jackal has been teasing Hyena too much and Hyena is determined to have his revenge. While Jackal is out hunting, Hyena hides in his hole to ambush him. When he returns home Jackal stops at some distance from his hole and shouts "Hole, how are you?" and when there is no reply shouts again "Hole, why don't you reply this evening?" Hyena thinks further silence will make Jackal suspicious, and so he makes a noise. Warned by this, Jackal runs away.'

The Tuareg are Muslim, but of relatively late conversion, and they have preserved some pre-Muslim beliefs. They believe in angels, which they call *andgelousen,* and in evil spirits inhabiting isolated rocks and trees. Many of them have heard that the earth goes round the sun, and that the Americans have been to the moon, but are not sure whether to believe such things. So they ask the holy men, who scold them for repeating such irreligious nonsense.

The basic social unit is a nuclear family of parents and unmarried children who inhabit one tent. Several tents of relatives and friends usually join up to form a camp. Members of a camp keep their animals separate from each other and can leave at any time. Camps are always changing in composition, as families join or leave, often as a result of quarrels between women, or because the men think better pasture is to be found elsewhere. Although Islam theoretically allows each man several wives the Tuareg are monogamous. Their women are generally rather independent, and have more sexual and economic freedom than is usual in the Muslim world. It is possible that the original Tuareg society was matriarchal and that traces of the old attitudes remain, despite the changes brought in by Islam.

Families belong to a clan. The clan in turn belongs to a social class or caste. Tuareg society has noble, vassal and religious classes, and blacksmith and slave castes. In the

At Bilma the salt saturated earth is kneaded with water and the salted water left to evaporate leaving a crude impure red salt, sold for animals.

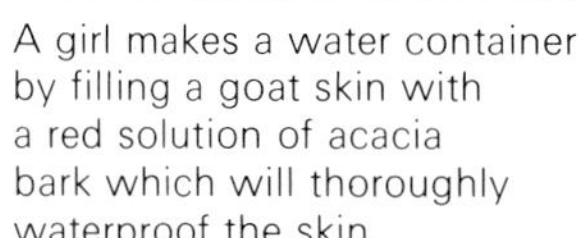

A girl makes a water container by filling a goat skin with a red solution of acacia bark which will thoroughly waterproof the skin.

A learned man or *marabut* leads a child through the Koran with the help of a wooden slate. *Marabuts* also help with marriages, illness and disputes.

past nobles fought to defend their herds and those of their vassals from raids, and lived partly from a tribute in animals and food from their vassals. Since the *pax gallica* in the Sahara in the 1930s such raiding has almost ceased, and nobles now live from their herds like the vassals.

Men of secular or religious learning are known as *marabuts*, and may be from any class, but there are also whole clans with a traditional reputation for holiness. The help of *marabuts* is sought for marriages, the settlement of disputes, curing illness and providing charms against bad luck and the devil. For these services *marabuts* are paid in animals, and consequently many of them are very rich.

Blinding white heat reflects from the sand as Tuareg load their camels with salt near Bilma before the annual caravan to Agades.

Tuareg blacksmiths are treated with some of the respectful scorn commonly given to those who work metals in primitive society. They are said to have a secret language, and at times fill important roles as advisers to chiefs. Blacksmiths are inventive and open to new ideas. They are paid for their work in kind, and are reputed to be spendthrifts.

The Tuareg live on the margin of the habitable world. Not only is the rainfall in most of their lands very low, but it is also very uncertain. Pasture depends on rain and so Tuareg herds have to move often to take advantage of the scarce and scattered vegetation. It is a hazardous and insecure life, and Tuareg behavior is dominated by this uncertainty. Their herds of camels, goats and sheep, with some cattle in the south, are managed to produce as much milk as possible; and milk, butter and cheese are the main Tuareg foods. Food shortages are made up for by selling young animals from the herds and by traveling north and south in caravans to the market towns on the desert edge. These caravans also serve to equip the Tuareg with those few products they need which they do not themselves produce – mainly tea, sugar, cloth and blankets. Tuareg also trade in salt from the mines at Taodenni and Amadror; and the annual salt caravan from Taodenni to Timbuctu, with thousands of camels carrying huge, gravestone-shaped blocks of salt, is one of the great sights of the Sahara, and an important part of the nomad economy.

In the Ahaggar, Tuareg still have plots of land and date palms, and they are increasingly cultivating these plots themselves now that their slaves and Haratin have been liberated.

Though the life of a nomad is difficult it does not usually demand great effort. For much of the year the animals graze on their own, and find their own way to water. Drawing water for the camp is a daily task, but it is often done by older children and it provides them with a chance to meet their friends from other camps. Women are usually occupied with leather or other handicraft work, but this can be done while they sit with their friends. Men spend some of their time visiting other camps and drinking sweet mint tea.

This apparently leisured life cannot conceal the real poverty of most Tuareg families, whose margin of safety from destitution or starvation is very narrow. An epidemic livestock disease may strike suddenly, or the animals may be scattered by a jackal in the night. In the dry season, entire herds are lost in sandstorms, or after a long trek when they arrive at a well which is dry. The Tuareg are very generous and unfailingly give animals and food to relatives and friends in such circumstances so that their society is criss-crossed with relationships arising from loans and gifts. The Tuareg go on caravan journeys of up to 1,700 miles across one of the most

To the delight of the whole camp two Kel Nan nobles fight a friendly joust with swords and spears in the quiet winter season.

Even the proud Tuareg must move with the times. Many of the boys go to boarding school now but they return home by camel for their vacations.

(Top) Perched on their high pommeled saddles riders urge their camels to greater speed by rhythmically pushing their feet against the camel's neck.

inhospitable deserts in the world, and on their return give away much of the meager merchandise in order to preserve this system of reciprocal obligations. A person in need is never abandoned.

In ways like this the life of the Tuareg is highly adapted to an extremely difficult environment, but it is now threatened by things beyond its control. Benevolent measures, like new wells or disease eradication, upset the delicate balance between the people and the natural resources which support them. In many places the Tuareg herds are overgrazing the Saharan and steppe vegetation, leaving themselves nowhere to go. There are plans for a trans-Saharan road, on which lorries would carry many of the things now taken by the Tuareg with their camel caravans. Tuareg caravans along the traditional routes are suddenly subject to new international frontiers and custom duties. By 1973 four years of drought along the southern edge of the Sahara had driven many Tuareg hundreds of miles south into pastures already crowded by other, often hostile herdsmen. Nomads are currently dying of starvation.

Most governments think nomads an anachronism, and see the future of the Sahara in terms of spectacular finds of oil, uranium and iron, with the nomads providing a cheap, plentiful and usefully close source of labor. If this happens a huge area will be lost to any form of agricultural production. The world will also lose a unique and finely adapted culture.

As she travels with her servant this young noble woman emerges from the tent behind her. She need not hide from anything but the sun.

People of Algeria

In turbulent Algeria conflict between Arab and Berber, nomad and farmer, was exacerbated by French colonialism. The result was war and revolution.

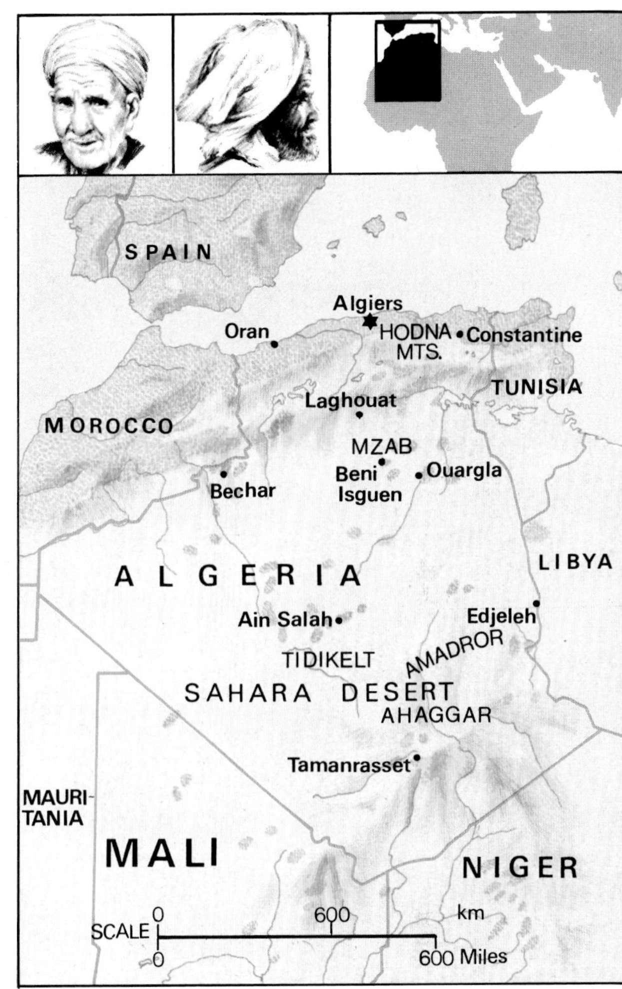

The history of Algeria is mirrored in the shifting frontier between nomadic herdsmen and the more settled mountain farmers. It is as true today as ever. Since the Roman period and even before, through the various Arab invasions and the French colonial period, these two irreconcilable ways of life have cut across the ethnic boundaries between the 3 million Berber and 12 million Arabs. Even among the original Berber population of North Africa, whom the Romans called Getuli, there was strife between farmers and nomadic herdsmen – and the nomads were dominant, restricting the peasant farmers to the mountainous areas.

Yet the presence of Rome and her well-guarded frontiers held the nomads back and enabled the expansion of the Berber farmers. Nor did the Arab conquest of North Africa in the 7th and 8th centuries AD destroy the relative rural prosperity developed under the Pax Romana. The nomads remained more or less restricted to the south of the old Roman frontiers, while the invading Arabs or arabized Berber settled in the cities. The Arab governors gradually, and in increasing num-

Close to the oasis where water is near the surface, men churn the soil into mud then shape bricks to bake in the sun.

(Bottom) With broad bladed mattocks, the best tool for scraping away sand, men dig an irrigation channel to a palm grove.

Whether on horseback or on foot, fierce tribesmen all over southern Algeria dance the warrior's dance as these men are doing in Timimoun.

bers, subdued and converted the Berber tribes to Islam. Their conversion, although superficial, was assisted by the attraction of loot from the conquest of Spain, and because Muslims were exempted from certain taxes.

For 300 years the Arab Empire in the Maghreb (the states of Algeria, Tunisia and Morocco) was a flowering reincarnation of the Roman Empire. The Arabs or arabized Berber populated the ancient cities or founded new ones, while the Berber peasants retained much of their rural prosperity. A true arabization of the Maghreb did not really get under way until the 11th century. Between then and the 14th century there was a great nomadic revival: Arabic tribesmen moving westwards attached themselves to the nomadic Berber tribes to the south of the old Roman frontiers. Among these tribes arabization – the adoption of Islam and Arab customs – was far less superficial than it had been earlier for the Berber farmers. Beginning in the 11th century the hordes of Beni Hilal, Beni Solayim, and the Makil moved northwards into the settled Berber countryside. The nomadic frontier was pushed forward. Villages disappeared, and the settled population shrank back into the mountains – where it has largely remained.

Today, the main Berber communities of Algeria are

The red mud-brick town of Timimoun is at the heart of the oasis. The white tower in the center is the tomb of a *marabut*, a holy man.

Through the scattered palms of In Salah oasis women carry split palm trunks, to be used as roofing rafters, on their heads.

concentrated in these mountain retreats – the Kabyles in the mountains of the Djurdjura and the Shawiya in the Aures and Hodna mountains. This is the paradox of Algeria (and most of the Maghreb). It is a land of poor overpopulated mountain areas inhabited by Berber-speaking farmers, with its rich coastal plain left under-populated. At least until the arrival of the French colonists in the 19th and 20th centuries the plains were given up to the nomadic Arab or arabized sheep herdsmen. With the Hilalian invasion, Algeria entered something of a dark period. In the west the nomads erased practically all trace of settled farming, while in the east the Berber farmers barricaded themselves into the Djurdjura, Aures and Hodna mountains of the Tellian Atlas.

In the Sahara, the history of the two Berber communities – the Mozabites and Tuareg – is a little different. About 375 miles south of Algeria, in the valley of the Mzab, are the five cities of the Mozabites. Founded in the 11th century, the cities of Ghardaia, Beni Isguen, Melika, Ben Noura, and El Ateuf held (in 1953) about 30,000 inhabitants of whom about half live in Ghardaia, the capital. The cities owe their existence to the Ibadites, a group of religious dissenters, who achieved a following of Berber. Refugees from orthodox Muslim persecution, they left their home in the High Atlas plains and came finally to the safer area of the Mzab. There in 1011 AD they founded El Ateuf. In the Mzab the rigidness, secrecy and self-denial of this puritanical faith has continued to flourish. But although the valley is an ideal retreat, the survival of the community has been dependent on trading elsewhere and sending the proceeds home, so that for nearly a thousand years Mozabite men have left their valley and gone north in search of trade. Today they are big landowners and investors (throughout the Maghreb and in Europe) and virtually in control of the national commerce.

As a boy, a Mozabite goes north to serve his apprenticeship in the commercial world and for the rest of his life will return to the Mzab at periodic intervals. Only when he has saved enough money, does he finally return to his family. The role of the women in Mozabite society is, however, quite different for there is the fundamental law that no Mozabite woman can leave the Mzab. The dogma that all Muslims are equal is expressed in the women's function as teachers, while their considerable authority makes them the guardians of not only the family hearth, but of the whole city. Among all these people, wealth and education have certainly given them

A sheep market at Ghardaia, a town founded in the 11th century by Mozabite Berber refugees, driven from their home in the High Atlas.

Mozabite women, forbidden by their strictly puritanical faith to leave the Mzab, stay at home while the men go out into the commercial world.

command of modern commercial practices. But above all else it is the spiritual strength of the community – particularly the insistence that the acquisition of wealth and the maintenance of the community is a moral duty in the glorification of God – that has enabled the Mzab to remain a theocracy and a society of equals.

The nomadic northern Tuareg people live in the south of Algeria, in the massif of Ahaggar and the adjoining Tassili-n-Ajjer. These Tuareg, the Kel Ahaggar and Kel Ajjer speak a Berber dialect *tamahak* and unlike other Berber-speaking peoples have a script known as *tifinagh*, the origin of which is unknown. Traditional Tuareg society was characterized by its class division into *imrad* vassals, and *ihaggaren* or nobles but the origin of this division, like that of the Tuareg as a whole, is obscure. This division may have arisen from two ancient and distinct Berber-speaking peoples meeting in the desert: a camel-breeding culture whose descendants are the noble *ihaggaren* and a goat-breeding culture, now the *imrad*.

Although there are only some 8,000 northern Tuareg, their traditional territory covers about 300,000 square miles in southern Algeria. Prior to their defeat by the French in 1902, the economy of the Kel Ahaggar had

Since Independence all the people, Arab and Berber – even the Beduin like this girl – have experienced a growing sense of nationalism.

been based largely on raiding in the lands around Ahaggar, and on the control of the main caravan routes passing eastwards through the Fezzan and westward from Timbuctu through the Tanezrouft. French encroachment not only impeded raiding but blocked the essential supply of dates and grain from the oases of Touat and Tidikelt to the north of Ahaggar, with the result that the Kel Ahaggar Tuareg were forced in 1896 to undertake their own caravans trading salt from the mines of Amadror for millet in southern Niger. From the 1920s these caravans became regular yearly events and were a mainstay of Tuareg economy.

Under a French military administration, whose policy was one of *laissez-faire,* most of the traditional activities and way of life of the Tuareg were protected. The authority of the Amenukal, the supreme chief, was reinforced. Pastoralism and migrations to the pastures of Tamesna in northern Niger were uninhibited. Cultivation by dark-skinned Harratin on a servile contract system expanded considerably, and slavery was condoned.

French presence in the Sahara effectively preserved the status quo. Their policy towards the various desert peoples – the nomadic Tuareg, Reguibat, Chaamba and other nomadic tribes – was traditionalist. Not until the development of mineral and hydro-carbon research in the 1950s did any significant development or change take place. In the north, however, the impact of colonialism differed considerably in that it reversed the process of de-ruralization that had resulted from the earlier nomad invasions, and sparked off a wave of migration to the colonized regions of Oran, the Mitidja, and Bone. The labor force required for the cultivation of these areas came from the settling of nomad tribes and the migration of highlanders, particularly the Kabyles. The migration of the Kabyles to Algiers gave the city a Berber majority.

During the centuries prior to French colonization, the nomadic and semi-nomadic Arab or arabized tribes had been fewer in number than the settled farming community, but more powerful in the political and military spheres. As the French colonists divided the more fertile regions into thousands of estates, they merely increased the population pressure on the nomads and caused whole tribes to shift towards a settled existence. And as the tribal chiefs tended to become big landowners so the common tribesman found himself joining – with the migrating Berber highlanders – the massive rural proletariat. Thus, while reversing the process set in motion by the nomadic invasions, the French brought about an overall change in the balance of the population.

In these years the French tended to see Maghrebian society rather superficially in terms of racial hostility, a struggle between Arabs and Berber, rather than in terms of an ideological conflict. They failed to see that many Berber tribes had in fact become arabized, and that Berber-speakers never regarded arabism as a hostile force, but rather as a cultural model. Arabic-speakers do exist but the way all these people see the world is interpreted through Islam. All Algerians, Arab and Berber (except the Mozabites), are Sunni Muslims.

An open-air café, reminiscent of French colonial times, is now the haunt of the new Algerians who have left the desert to live in the towns.

The Berber's lack of interest in separatism was clearly manifested in the growth of Algerian nationalism. This culminated in the War of Independence between 1954 and 1962. Indeed Berber, especially Kabyles, were in the forefront of the nationalist movement, but Berberism never became a major issue.

In the decade following Independence, Algeria has experienced extensive changes. Throughout the entire country (even among the remote Tuareg) there is a growing awareness of and indentification with Algeria – tribalism in its broadest sense is giving way to nationalism. The government has concentrated on the development of the more underdeveloped regions, notably the Berber highland areas and the Sahara as a whole. While development in Kabylia has prevented any serious Berber dissidence and given the government a degree of popularity, development policies in the vast Saharan region – the forgotten area of Algeria – have not been accepted readily by all the desert people. Among the Tuareg especially there has been resistance to the modern encapsulating system. In recent years, the Tuareg land has been taken over by their former Harratin contract-cultivators. Slaves have been emancipated. Caravan trade has been seriously impeded by bad harvests in the Niger and the imposition of a quota system and droughts have reduced the camel and goat herds to a poor, almost skeletal condition. Government policies and ecological forces have created a social revolution in Ahaggar. By the 1970s Tuareg children were attending the boarding school in the administrative capital of Tamanrasset. Men were looking for wage-earning opportunities. The number of nomadic camps was dwindling as more and more became settled in the small cultivation centers. In the small plots and agricultural co-operatives (set up after 1965) one can now find Kel Ahaggar working alongside their former slaves and Harratin cultivators.

Berbers of the Atlas
Morocco

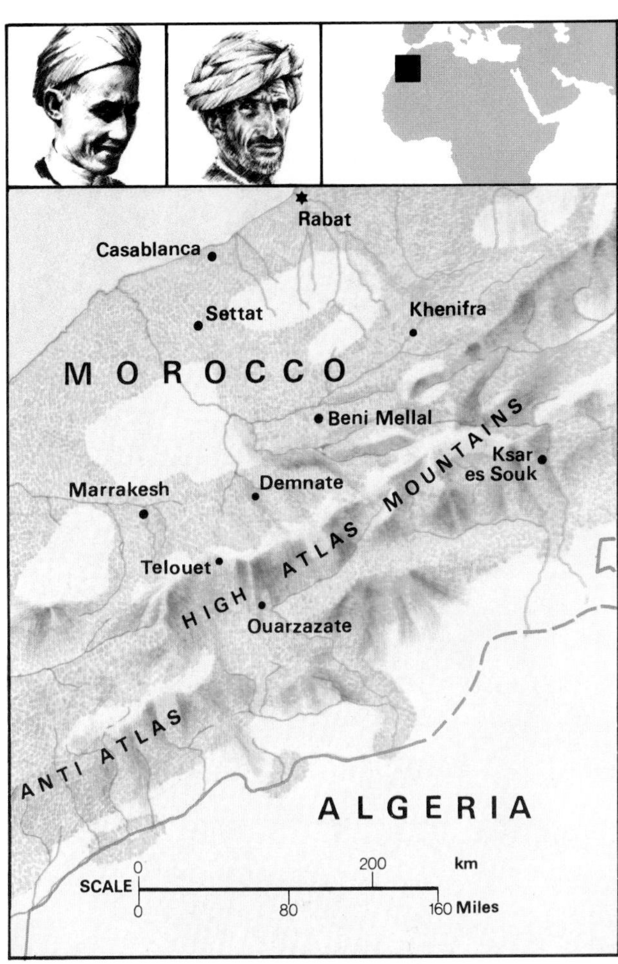

The vastness of northern Africa, now Muslim and predominantly Arab, was once the domain of the Berber – a people whose origins are obscure, whose history cannot be unveiled beyond the arrival of Islam and whose language is at most very distantly related to Arabic. Today these Berber, who still speak the Berber tongue, live in the less accessible regions of northern Africa, mainly in the deserts or the mountains. It can be assumed that these people are the remnant of a once far larger group. In appearance many Berber resemble southern Europeans more than they resemble Arabs. No doubt other ancient colonists of North Africa – the Carthaginians, Romans, Vandals and Byzantines – each contributed to the composition of the population. But there is little or no Berber folk memory of those times. When the Arabs crossed the plains of northern Africa they transformed Berber culture and today the Berber see their own past as inextricable from the history of Islam.

Within 100 years of the death of Mohammed in 632 AD the forces of the Arab caliphate had already embarked on a career of conquest in North Africa. Before long the Muslims covered the entire territory from Egypt to

Berber village women are freer than their urban Arab sisters. They must help in the fields and so cannot be kept behind walls and veils.

Berber of the Atlas Morocco

Unveiled Berber women make the most of their pretty faces. Their marital status is indicated by the way in which they tie their head-dress.

The fire is the center of Berber family life. If the family is a small one men women and children will all sit round it together.

Settled Berber, who farm in irrigated fields, leave for work in the morning and return in the evening, commuting on their donkeys and mules.

Each Berber family has its own fortress-like home in the village. Strongly built, these houses can be up to three stories high.

Morocco, almost all of which had been the Berber's homeland. With the invaders came Islam, and in due course the new religion replaced the Christianity imposed by earlier Graeco-Roman occupiers. Arabization was under way. But this initial conquest was mainly political. The Berber often revolted against the invaders and succeeded in re-establishing their own dynasties while accepting Islam as their religion. Only in the 11th century did a mass immigration of Arabs begin. These 'Hilalian' invaders were Beduin Arabs, nomads, intolerant of both urban and agricultural civilization. They are often accused of destroying the centuries-old balance which the Berber had achieved between animal husbandry and agriculture. The process of arabization continued, and today many original inhabitants are now so completely arabized that they can no longer be called Berber.

The Berber language is now spoken only in a large number of pockets stretching from the western desert of Egypt to the Atlantic coast of Morocco, and from the Mediterranean to the Niger bend. Most of these pockets are in the desert or mountainous regions which were less accessible to the invaders and their influences.

Although the Berber can today be distinguished only by their Berber speech, not all Berber speakers are Berber. A large Berber-speaking Jewish population once inhabited the Atlas region. They were mainly traders and artisans who lived under Berber protection, and most of them have emigrated to Israel since 1948. There are also many Berber speaking negro groups, mainly oasis cultivators and artisans, whose origins are obscure. They are attached to Berber tribes, but do not enjoy full rights of tribal citizenship.

Berber have a strong sense of identification with their clan and tribe; they also have some sense of regional belonging. What they conspicuously lack is a sentiment of Berber nationhood. The Berber are almost invariably rural tribesmen. When they become urbanized, as so many have done recently, they soon lose their Berber language and identity.

The largest pocket of Berber speakers is in the Atlas mountains in Morocco. The territory of the Berber covers an area corresponding approximately to three parallel mountain ranges: the Middle Atlas, the High Atlas and the Anti-Atlas. On the southern, Sahara side, the semi-deserts and oases of the mountains are inhabited by a mixture of peoples, some Arabic-speaking and some Berber-speaking. But the mountains themselves present a large and solid Berber block. Here Arabic is spoken only on ritual occasions.

Within this large region, there are two groups of dialects, roughly corresponding to two ways of life. In the north-eastern part (the Middle Atlas, eastern and central High Atlas and Jebel Saghro), there is a group which calls itself the Beraber. In the western High Atlas and the Anti-Atlas, there is the group known as Shluh. The difference between the ways of life of these

In the village of Haodeguine two Ait Haddidou girls gossip together while one of them spins wool which she will knit later.

(Bottom) The spices of the Berber market can be used to garnish food or women. Henna is a particular favorite for dyeing the hair red.

A Berber child recites his Arabic lesson; his own language has no script. The tuft of hair on his head is to help Allah take him when he dies.

two groups is one of degree rather than of kind. The Shluh are more settled than the Beraber. Neither group is in any real sense nomadic, but seasonal migrations are far more important in the lives of the Beraber than among the Shluh. From tribe to tribe the importance of agriculture and pastoralism varies, but all of these people depend on a number of resources – irrigated fields fed by irrigation ditches from local rivers; non-irrigated fields dependent on rainfall; forests which provide fodder for flocks; and pasture which depends on rain, and even more on melted snow in the spring.

Among the tribes there are various complex arrangements for the use and dispersal of these resources. Irrigated fields are owned individually, but tribal customary law makes selling to strangers difficult or impossible. Within tribal territory a man could once extend his fields simply by plowing up woodland; but today anti-erosion regulations prohibit this. Among tribes dependent on forest for fodder, the trees may be owned by individual families. Pasture rights are defined in terms of tribes and clans, with provisions to ensure that some pasture remains unused until the end of the season. Some tribes, while traveling with their livestock, use tents; others use permanent shacks, caves or rudimentary shelters, part stone wall, part tent covering, part tree.

There was always trade between the tribes of this region. Salt and dates came from the south, other goods from the coast. Besides this there was always exchange of the surpluses of both agricultural and animal produce. There is no lack of economic sophistication among these tribesmen: trade has long been conducted through the medium of money, and the obligations of ritual hospitality associated with these tribes co-exists with an intelligent use of market mechanisms. Weekly tribal markets are important institutions, and places of religious pilgrimage often combine a ritual and an economic role. In the days of feuding, insecurity and strong mutual suspicion, members of different tribes would

Near Msemrir, in the upper Dades valley, this woman is cooking a goat's head. She is a member of the nomadic Ait Morrhad tribe.

pair off, so that each could be safe in the other's territory – even when there was no one else to keep the Sultan's peace. Markets, however, remained potentially dangerous places, where feuds were often started or fanned into life.

In the Atlas mountains, the Berber have collective storehouses, also used as forts. These are generally either square towers – very rarely circular – or they are built in a cave. There is a single door and beyond it a courtyard onto which the many cells open out, dark holes in the walls, haphazardly placed, with poles and wooden ledges protruding by which the villagers may climb to their supplies. Each of the families of the clan which owns the fort has its own cubicle and one villager is entrusted with the key to the main entrance and the role of guardian. When the tribe was at war with any of its neighbors the entire community could take refuge inside their fort. It is also useful for families away at a distant pasture and cannot spare a son to guard the home. While the family cares for the flocks, the family possessions are safe in the store house. The fort remains in use in the Atlas mountains even today, though the Moroccan government has imposed its authority and no longer permits inter-tribal warfare.

The collective storehouses are often buildings of great elegance and beauty, and the same is also true of other Berber buildings, notably in the southern and western parts of the mountains. They use various techniques, mainly stamped mud reinforced by timber but sometimes dry stone or bricks, to build tower-like dwellings, often decorated with abstract relief designs. These are intended to ward off the evil eye.

The ideal of Berber family life is the extended family group. Brothers will often carry on working their father's land together rather than divide it between them on his death. Where small families exist, a man and his wife tend to eat together and share more of the activities of day to day life: in larger families the worlds of men and women tend to be segregated. The Berber woman, however, is in many ways freer than her urban Arab sister. To a certain extent this is the consequence of rural life and poverty: the woman must help in the fields, and therefore cannot be concealed behind walls and veils. In the mountains the bride-price a man must pay for a woman is negligible. The real expense of a wedding is the feast, and this falls upon the groom and his family. Only since 1956 have women been entitled to inherit wealth in property from their fathers, for in the past this was divided only between the sons, though lip-service has always been paid to the koranic obligation to give a half share to the daughter.

The political life of the Berber has generally been egalitarian. Decisions were taken by an assembly which included most male heads of households. Leadership was often elective, and the chief held his position for one year only – when the year had passed the position fell to

(Over page) Ait Haddidou Berber gather for the feast of the sheep to pray for the fertility of their flocks in the Upper Dades valley.

In the Atlas mountains flour is still made the traditional way: the grain is placed on one rounded stone, and ground with another.

the head of another clan in the tribe. One rule required that when the candidates on any given occasion were from one clan the electors were drawn from another. The same system operated at different levels: from choosing village headmen, to electing the chiefs of larger groupings. This system was evidently designed to prevent the emergence of a single, all-powerful individual, and in some regions it achieved this end. Although some individual men or Berber families were richer or more powerful than others, no deep and permanent social stratification ever crystallized.

Nevertheless in other regions it was sometimes possible for ruthless individuals to acquire great personal power. Often they began as modest elected chiefs, but by skillfully manipulating clan rivalries they succeeded in building up remarkable fiefs for themselves. These petty tyrannies, however, did not lead to any real stratification between rulers and oppressed peasantry. The dynastic succession troubles and the impinging European world, culminating in the establishment of the French protectorate over Morocco in 1912, were particularly fertile backgrounds for such enterprises. In the western High Atlas mountains three great robber-baronies emerged. Of the three the most famous was that of Glawi, Pasha of Marrakesh. His power was the only one to survive as an empire within an empire. But upon the recovery of Moroccan independence during the winter of 1955 it collapsed.

The most characteristic legal institution of traditional Berber society, one which survived till 1955, was trial by collective oath. This is a procedure in which the justice of an accusation is decided by making the accused and his kinsmen testify solemnly, at a sacred place, that he is innocent. These 'co-jurors' were not witnesses, for they did not necessarily know whether or not the accusation was justified. Rather, they were like guarantors, who by their oath 'dared' the supernatural to punish them all if their testimony was false. Despite the apparent illogicality of a system which makes the kinsmen of the accused an automatic jury, it worked quite well. It enabled a cohesive and decided group to swear one of its members out of an accusation – but in the anarchic conditions which prevailed, there was little use in pursuing such an accusation anyway, and the procedure at least enabled the accuser to withdraw without loss of face. The oath could on the other hand place considerable strain on an unsure or disunited group, and often led to a 'conviction' and the payment of a fine. It encouraged groups to police their own members.

In Berber villages, formal and literate Islam is represented by the scribe, generally an outsider to the village, who looks after the mosque and teaches the children prayers and Koranic wisdom. But he is not a priest, either in the sense of possessing a special sacramental status or of being backed by some religious hierarchy. Far more influential than the scribe are the hereditary

This traditional garment of home-knitted striped cloth could once be seen all over the Atlas. It is now being replaced by imported clothes.

In winter heavy snow often covers the mountains for many weeks. This does not stop the movements of Berber shepherds or caravan traders.

(Bottom) The Ait Haddidou, one of the Berber tribes, invented this game which bears an uncanny resemblance to hockey.

holy men, *igurramen*, who in most cases also claim to be *shurfa*, descendants of the prophet. In the sanctuary of the shrine it was they who traditionally supervized the collective oaths and tribal elections, who ratified agreements and generally acted as mediators and arbitrators between tribes.

It is natural to suppose that they are survivors of a pre-Islamic Berber institution. This has taken on a Muslim identity through these holy men or 'saints' attaching their lineages to the prophet's. If this were taken literally their ancestry would make them Arabs – especially as it is their belief that they should only marry among themselves. Nevertheless, the 'saints' and their customs are as fully Berber as that of the lay tribesmen.

In modern times the social history of the two main Berber regions has diverged. The population in the south-western part seems to have reached saturation point. Now it is from this region that many people migrate to Moroccan towns and to Europe as traders or temporary laborers. In the Middle Atlas range the population pressure is less acute and there is even room for further agricultural expansion.

The political role of the two major areas in independent Morocco has also diverged. The migrant traders from the south-west have (in spite of their successful trading activities) tended to find political expression through the leftist UNFP party. This party represents their interests against their most important rivals, the old-established commercial families from Fes, now often transplanted in Casablanca.

By contrast the Berbers from the Middle Atlas regions have been prominent in the new Morocco as soldiers and administrators, and for a time they seemed to be the most important pillar of the monarchy. In a new form, they seemed to reproduce the traditional Moroccan pattern, in which the monarchy draws its support from privileged tribes who are its sword-arm. There was a certain irony in the fact that these traditionally anarchic tribes, who in the past had done so much to trouble the peace of the realm, had now become its main support. But during the abortive military coups of 1971 and 1972, a remarkable number of these supposedly loyal royalist Berber officers had been involved in the rebellion, including the most famous Berber soldier of independent Morocco, Oufkir. The events of those years suggest that the honeymoon between the Berber and the Moroccan monarchy may have ended.

The Berber who remain in the mountains still live as small farmers and pastoralists, still familiar with the old tribal affiliations when the laws were in the keeping of tribal assemblies and the hereditary holy men. Those who have moved to the cities, away from the mountains, as laborers or traders, soldiers and administrators, have tended to become arabized. But this is just a continuation of the historical process which began when Islam first conquered the Berber.

People of Morocco

Although most of Morocco's population is rural, its charm and attraction lies in cities like Marrakesh, famed for mystery and romance.

All Muslim boys are circumcised, from the king's son at the Palace, to the humblest peasant child at a local village clinic.

Beggars are still a common sight in Morocco. Often crippled or deformed, they rely on the generosity of passers-by for their living.

(Left) The tanners of Fes have been using the same methods for generations. They enter the dying vats and work the leather with their hands.

Most Moroccans, whether Muslims or Jews, are caucasoid or 'white' but there are also negroid or 'black' people. Almost all the 'black' Moroccans are Muslims and originated, whether in the last few centuries or much earlier, from the regions south of the Sahara with whom Morocco once had important commercial relations. Among the 'white' Moroccans there are often physical differences. The Berber of the Rif mountains in the north, for example, often have unusually light complexions and there are some with red hair and blue eyes, features rare among those of Arab descent.

Visible physical differences distinguish the 'black' peoples of Morocco from the rest of the native inhabitants, but the distinction has been blurred through centuries of intermingling. Moroccans of negro origin or of mixed negro and Berber blood mostly live in the south of Morocco where they are often called Haratin. In the past the Haratin and darker skinned people were considered inferior. And the fact that Haratin often worked in such traditionally despised professions as tanning leather and working iron was a further sign of their low social status. Today there is little discrimination. Most 'black' Moroccans, however, are among the poorest people of both town and country. Often they are believed to hold unusual powers, both magical and healing, and they dominate the 'healing brotherhoods' which use ecstatic religion to heal mental and physical illness. Many 'black' Moroccans in central and northern regions, particularly the towns, are the descendants of slaves, concubines and mercenaries brought into Morocco by the sultans and by the urban and rural élite to be members of their entourages and personal bodyguards. In pre-colonial Morocco 'black' slaves often achieved powerful positions in the armies of the sultans, where they were frequently entrusted with high command.

Moroccan Jews are distinguished from other Moroccans by their religion. There were Jews in Morocco under the Romans but many of these were probably Berber who became converted to Judaism. There were even tribes of Jews, or rather Jewish Berber, in the Maghreb during the 7th and 8th centuries. Between the 8th and 15th centuries many Jews arrived from Spain to settle in Morocco. They played an important part in developing trade between Europe and North Africa. Some achieved positions of wealth and power under the Muslim leaders but these were always a minority. Most worked as petty traders and craftsmen in the towns or, more rarely, in the country. As craftsmen the Jews were renowned as jewelers and goldsmiths – a reputation they still have. They also acted as money lenders for usury was forbidden by Islam. As the Jews were generally mistrusted and despised they tended to live apart from the Muslims. Traditionally they had their own quarter or ghetto, the *mellah*. And when they left their ghetto they were supposed to wear distinctive black *jellabas* (hooded gowns) and skullcaps. Throughout the 19th century, and

Most of the tanners live in a special quarter of Fes. When unmanned and idle, the dye pits make an unusual and eerie landscape.

(Bottom) Newly dyed wool hangs up to dry in a Moroccan village. It will soon be expertly woven into an intricately patterned carpet.

Important centers like Fes, Marrakesh and Rabat now have a 'new town' where the well-off live, as well as the old section, the *medina*.

increasingly in the present century, the rural Jewish population have migrated to the towns, particularly those on the west coast like Casablanca. In 1948, at the time of the creation of the State of Israel there were 250,000 Jews in Morocco, but steady emigration has since drastically reduced that number. The majority – the elderly, the uneducated and the poor – have left for Israel; many of the wealthiest went to Europe and Canada. Those that remain are usually well off and well-educated but are becoming increasingly isolated from the mainstream of life in Morocco. Today they no longer wear their traditional garb and are superficially indistinguishable from Muslims in their western clothes or ordinary *jellabas*. And they are no longer confined to their ghetto. Most Muslim Moroccans, however, still regard the Jews with suspicion and even hostility especially since the aggravation of relations between Israel and the Arab states.

The European community in Morocco is essentially a result of the colonial period and consists largely of Catholic French and Spanish expatriates. The Spanish live mainly in the northern towns in what was the Spanish zone of the Protectorate, while the French predominate in what was formerly the French zone.

Most of the large towns and the bulk of Morocco's population are in the western half of the country. Casablanca, on the Atlantic coast, is a major industrial center and Morocco's largest city with a population of over a million. The traditional royal capitals of the sultans are Marrakesh in the south and Meknes and Fes in the north. In the summer the king and his family go to their summer palace in Tangier on the Mediterranean coast. The modern administrative capital is Rabat built at the mouth of the River Bou-Regreg, 60 miles north of Casablanca. Across the river from Rabat is her twin town, Sala, notorious in earlier times as a base for the pirates and corsairs of the 'Barbary coast'. In the urban areas most people are Muslim and speak Arabic.

The numbers of Jews and Europeans in the towns are declining and it is likely that in the next few decades Morocco will become religiously homogenous, in the towns as well as in the countryside.

Many towns in Morocco reflect the existence of Muslims, Jews and Europeans in the way they are laid out. The traditional Muslim town *(medina)* was walled with a gate which was locked at sunset. Inside the *medina* the Jews had their own ghetto. When the French and Spanish colonized Morocco they built their own towns outside the *medina*. These new modern towns display every variety of European architecture with rows of handsome buildings ranged along broad tree-lined avenues. So important centers like Fes, Meknes, Marrakesh, Teutan, Tangier and Rabat all have a 'new town' and an 'old town'. Today most wealthier Moroccans tend to live in the 'new town' while the poorer Moroccans live mainly in the *medina* with its narrow alleyways,

The *medinas* are known for their covered souks where tourists collect souvenirs and the local people buy food and implements.

Local arts and crafts are spread out alongside a large variety of foodstuffs for passers-by to feast their senses on.

covered markets, ancient mosques and houses built round hidden courtyards. In the covered markets Moroccan craftsmen work at their traditional crafts – copper and brass beating, furniture making and leather-work.

Three-quarters of Morocco's people live in the country. Since 1960 the government has divided the rural areas into 'rural communes' for the purposes of local administration. Most rural Moroccans, however, still think of themselves as belonging to a particular tribe rather than to a specific locality. Over 750 tribes have been recorded. The colonial administrations of both the French and Spanish used the existing tribal divisions for administrative purposes and so the tribes remain as independent social, cultural and sometimes linguistic entities well in to the second half of the 20th century. This is so despite the fact that the social and political structure of the 19th century Moroccan state – in which the central government was continually involved in establishing and maintaining its control over the tribes – has been transformed into a modern state where tribal politics in the old sense no longer exist. Rural Moroccans still consider themselves as tribesmen belonging to a particular tribe or group of tribes. They claim membership of their tribe by virtue of their supposed descent from the original founder. Each tribe has a distinct identity, usually expressed in terms of kinship and descent from the common ancestor. Many tribal groups are known as Beni X, Ulad Y or Ait Z, all of these being words in Arabic or Berber which mean 'children of' X, Y and Z.

Most rural Moroccans should be regarded as peasants rather than tribesmen. ('Tribesmen' suggests, often wrongly, isolation, 'primitiveness' and a certain type of political structure.) They all, whether farmers, herdsmen or fishermen, concentrate on producing enough food for their needs. They also market their produce, pay taxes and buy goods from outside the region they live in and even from outside Morocco. Sixty-five per cent of the active labor force is involved in agriculture, livestock raising and fishing, while one Moroccan in thirty is a

In a small Fes clinic, parents bring their boys to be circumcised. The queue winds round the building and up the hill behind it.

Circumcision is traditionally performed by barbers. They operate with scissors and there is no anaesthetic and no antiseptic.

Morocco is the last monarchy in North Africa. Royal processions are festive occasions complete with special incense burners.

small trader or merchant, many of whom live in small market centers or villages. Nearly all the people in the rural areas, whether peasant, farm laborer, livestock-breeder, shepherd, fisherman or trader are Muslims and speak either Berber or Arabic as their first language. The majority are illiterate or semi-literate and their accents, if they speak Arabic, distinguish them clearly from the townspeople. They also interpret Islam and the practices of Islam differently; they worship saints, use rhythmic drumming and dancing to achieve ecstatic states and revere holy men. In the towns people tend to respect religious learning highly and consider intermediaries between man and Allah as deviations from the ideal.

Although it is language that essentially divides the Moroccans into Berber and Arabs, the history of Arab-Berber relations and differences is long and complex. The origins of the Berber are a mystery. Although they arrived in North Africa before the Arabs little is known of where they came from or when. What is certain, however, is that by the 5th century BC, when Carthage had become the center of a vast trading empire, Berber tribes already lived in the hinterland. After the destruction of Carthage by the Romans in 146 BC the Berber came nominally under Roman rule. The Roman occupation lasted for 400 years during which time some Berber adopted Latin and other aspects of Roman culture.

Next came the Vandals who crossed from Spain and conquered most of the Roman-held territory. But they were not the last. A hundred years later in 533 AD the Byzantines took the Maghreb, destroying the Vandal state. The Berber at this time were either settled farmers in the mountains and plains, or nomads or semi-nomads in the steppes and high plateaux and on the desert fringes.

The next conquerors were the Arabs. Between 704 and 711 AD they overran the western parts of the Maghreb despite Berber resistance, bringing the Islamic faith and the Arabic language with them. Thousands of Berber were nominally converted to Islam and, although their knowledge of Islam doctrine remained slight during the early centuries of Arab rule, they adhered fervently to their new faith. During the following 8th, 9th and 10th centuries the Berber became involved in a series of religious and political struggles which divided the Maghreb into warring states.

The 11th to 15th centuries saw the rise of three dynasties, all of them founded by Berber tribesmen: the Almoravids, the Almohads and the Merinids. The first two of these originated as reformist religious movements. This series of tribal states evolved out of rural Berber society – the Almoravids and the Merinids were originally nomadic herders, the Almohads settled farmers. The centers of their political and religious power were the cities they controlled. These tribal states were Islamic in the sense that their rulers championed the cause of political unity in the name of Islam, but the rulers of these states were illegitimate in a strict Islamic state for they were not Arabs and could not be descended from the prophet. For this reason their religious authority was questionable.

The expansion of the Christian Portuguese and Spanish into North Africa towards the end of the 15th century coincided with the rise of the sherifian cult in the Maghreb. The sherifs were holy men who claimed descent from the prophet. They came increasingly to be regarded by Moroccans as symbols of the ideal of Moroccan unity, of disenchantment with tribal leadership and of determination to resist foreign armies which threatened Morocco and its faith. The two dynasties which have ruled Morocco since the 16th century, the Saadians (1510-1603) and the Alawites (1668-1973), were both Sherifian dynasties. Gradually, over four and a half centuries, the central government with 'Arab' sherifian authority gained control of the towns and cities and of the tribes that lived near them. And these people became more 'arabized' while the people in the remote areas remained Berber-speaking and tribal. When in the first quarter of the 20th century the French took control of

On the occasion of the prince's circumcision a week of festivities was proclaimed. Berber horsemen rode into Fes to display their skills.

In a high-class café an ornately-costumed orchestra entertains customers with favorite tunes played on traditional instruments.

Though more adequately covered than her Egyptian counterpart, this Moroccan belly-dancer is no less expert in her art.

On the occasion of a national holiday Berber girls, distinct with their heavy gold jewelry and tatooed faces, come into Fes.

Morocco and established colonial rule they attempted to divide the Muslim population more strictly into Arabs and Berber, developing different legal and administrative structures to deal with each group. This attempt failed and indeed helped to create and consolidate a new spirit of Muslim Moroccan nationalism.

Today roughly 40 per cent of Moroccans speak Berber, but it is difficult to be precise. There are many who speak Berber at home and Arabic at work or in the market place. Arabic is, however, the dominant language of Morocco: the language of religion, of bureaucracy, of the market place, of the television, radio and newspapers. Groups are also sometimes distinguished on the basis of origins; but this produces anomalies for there are 'Berber' tribes that now speak only Arabic and 'Arab' tribes that speak Berber, and it is probable that the great majority of all groups today regarded as 'Arabs' and speaking Arabic were originally Berbers or at least contain a 'mixed' population. If the distinction is primarily linguistic it is important to recognize that sometimes this form of distinction coincides with other differences, but sometimes alternative forms of cleavage and differentiation blur this linguistic distinction, such as the opposition between townsman and countryman, between settled farmer and nomadic pastoralist, or between rich and poor. And while the Arabic spoken in Morocco varies slightly from region to region, it may be considered as a single dialect. The three main Berber groups each have their own dialect. These groups are: the Riffians of the Rif mountains in the north, the groups of the Middle Atlas and of the central High Atlas and Sahara who speak Tamazight, and the High and Anti-Atlas groups who speak Tashilhit.

The southern Berber, the Shluh of the western High Atlas and Anti-Atlas, speak Tashilhit. Many of the Shluh of the plains and foothills bordering the mountains also speak Arabic, and Arabic-speaking tribes intermingled with Shluh in the southern areas. The Shluh are settled farmers who live in stone or pounded-earth houses concentrated in small villages with fortified storehouses or granaries. In the high mountains they farm using irrigation and terracing and keep sheep. They grow different crops depending on altitude. In the valleys the farmers keep mainly cattle and goats. West and south of the mountains the country becomes drier, agriculture more hazardous and goats become the commonest form of livestock. Further south the people are nomadic pastoralists. Some of the nomadic groups still migrate considerable distances into the Sahara. The tribes north of the Dra'a are concentrated in oases and live in fortified villages (*ksur*). Towards the south Arabic is spoken more often, although some Berber-speaking groups are nomadic

Berber tribesmen, who travel with their flocks according to the seasons of the year, prepare themselves to go to a village market.

and some nomadic groups are bilingual.

The Berabers, a group of Berber, live principally in the mountains of central Morocco, in the eastern High Atlas, their southern slopes, and the Middle Atlas. They speak Tamazight but some southern groups also speak Arabic. The Beraber are semi-nomads. They winter with their sheep and goats in the warmer plains or steppes and move to higher pastures in the mountains during spring and summer. In their winter quarters the Beraber maintain permanent villages with fortified communal granaries and surrounding farmlands. To the south, in the pre-Saharan steppe, the granary (*ighrem* or *tighremt*) becomes a strongly fortified village.

North of Beraber country is the Jebala-Ghomara-Rif region. Almost all the tribes in this northern region, whose center is the Rif mountains of the Mediterranean coast, are Berber by origin and culture, although the Jebala and Ghomara tribes in the west now largely speak Arabic. The tribes of the Rif, who have retained their Berber dialect, are settled farmers who grow wheat and barley and cultivate small orchards of figs, almonds and olives on barren hillsides, and keep goats and cattle. In the past they have emigrated seasonally to work on

This craftsman uses both hands and feet to manipulate his traditional lathe. The result of his effort will be a fine table.

Hundreds of shepherds with thousands of sheep and goats miraculously manage both to keep their flocks together and sell or barter successfully.

Both camel and donkey are
used as draft animals by
the oasis tribes who live
on the dates and other crops
they grow in southern Morocco.

French farms in Algeria. Today many migrate to western Europe. Riffians live in small villages of mud- and stone-built houses or else in scattered homesteads.

The nomadic Arabic-speakers are either sheep-herders, such as the tribes of the north-east and of the eastern high plateaux, or camel-herders who live mainly in the far south on the fringes of the desert and into the Sahara. These nomadic groups usually have special social and economic relations with a particular group of cultivators with whom they exchange crops and other goods for animal products. The sedentary Arabic-speakers live predominantly in the western coastal plains of the Gharb and the Sebu river valley in the north, and the plateaux and plains of the Meseta, the Tadla, the Rehamna, the Djebilet and the Hauz further south.

The life of all these groups is dominated by the changing seasons: the agricultural cycle or the requirements of the flocks and herds. The farmers, for example, hold marriages and other feasts in the slack period after the harvest, when there are crops and grain in abundance. Work starts again in earnest in the autumn when the men start plowing for the new season. But these people of the countryside are not isolated and cut off from contact with the other parts of Morocco, for there are trucks and buses as well as the radio. And perhaps most important there are local and regional markets where the people flock, not merely to sell their produce and to purchase goods from elsewhere in Morocco and from abroad, but also to meet each other, to exchange news and gossip, to discuss local and national politics and to be entertained by visiting snake charmers and story tellers or helped by herbal doctors and dentists.

Through the market network, as well as through the political parties, migration, the administration and other means, the people of the rural areas are linked to other parts of Morocco, particularly to the towns. The petty traders from the Sus valley have, for example, established elaborate networks of small shops throughout Morocco, but most notably in Casablanca. Particular tribes tend to specialize in particular trades: the Ammeln are usually tobacconists and grocers, and some of the Ida u Gnidif have challenged the traditional craftsmen of Fes in leather and textile trade. As the rural areas become ever more closely integrated within the national economy and political system, so life in the countryside is transformed. The linguistic and tribal divisions become less significant. In some contexts, they are replaced by other divisions, between capitalist farmers and agricultural laborers, for example. In other contexts, as in the case of the Sussi traders, tribal connections take on new functions.

The people in the rural areas of Morocco are not backward, 'traditional' tribesmen but, like those in the towns, part of a changing 20th century state, and the cultural, linguistic, ethnic and economic patterns that exist today in the countryside are also undergoing change, even as one observes them.

Some of the Berber tribes of Morocco live in towns and villages completely surrounded by thick, heavy walls.

The walls protect both the crops of each individual family and the village as a whole from possible attack by other tribes.

Sanusi
Libya

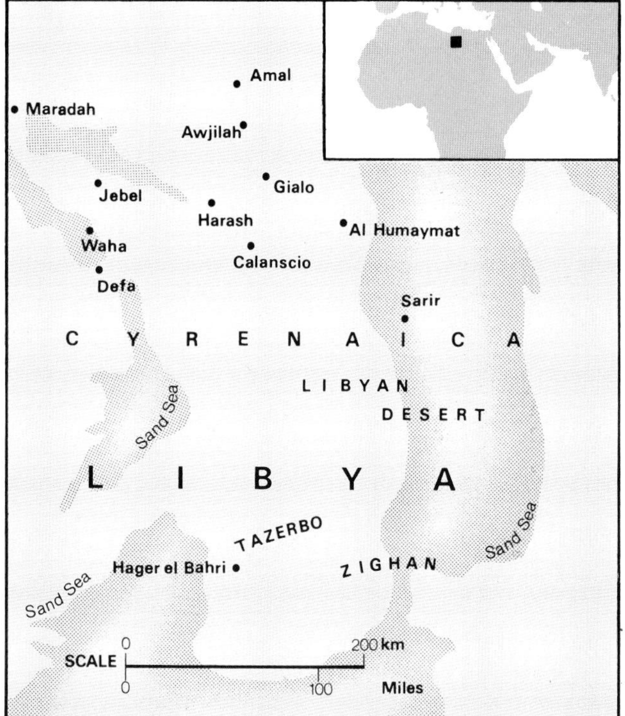

When the Grand Sanusi first came to preach in Cyrenaica, north-eastern Libya, in the early 1830s, he found the Beduin tribes without law or effective government, but with common values and habits and a community of life which crossed all tribal boundaries. The Grand Sanusi had been born in Algeria and had already gained a reputation as a leader of his own Islamic Order of Sufis. The Beduin to whom he preached were simple people leading the austere and monotonous life of the tents, with that savage character which has so often been portrayed, but also with those noble qualities which have seldom failed to evoke admiration from men who have lived among them. They were profoundly ignorant of the outside world of the mid-19th century and also – which is what touched the heart of the Grand Sanusi – about the faith of their fathers. The Beduin professed Islam, but they were almost totally ignorant of its doctrinal content, rites or ritual and moral duties. In Cyrenaica, isolated by hundreds of miles of desert on three sides, the conditions were particularly favorable to the growth of an order of Islam which was austere without being fanatical, which could embrace and become part of the tribal structure and which offered a political organization through which the Beduin could express themselves.

The Grand Sanusi came to the Beduin tribes of Cyrenaica and was not appealing to a pagan people to embrace Islam, but was asking a Muslim people to show in their lives the faith they professed. It was his achievement to give their religion organized form and direction, and by so doing to exercise an influence on their morals. If these same Beduin today seem to neglect their religious duties and to be ignorant, loud and lawless by peasant or urban standards, it can be imagined that they were troublesome indeed before the Grand Sanusi softened the harshness of their customs. In effect, the order he created among them became more than a religious order, it evolved into a political order that united the tribes through its lodges and bound them to a path whose principles were simply 'to do good and avoid evil'.

Early in his life, the Grand Sanusi had affiliated himself to a number of Muslim orders before founding his own. He was not peculiar among Sufis, yet his later teachings were not a mere amalgam of the tenets of earlier orders; they may not have been original, but they formed a consistent and carefully thought out way of life. He did not choose Cyrenaica as his field of labor, but rather was compelled to settle there for a time because the road to the west was closed by the French in Algeria, and the road to the east by the authorities in Cairo and Mecca who were jealous of the success of his teachings. Their real objections were that his Order threatened the prestige and privileges of these authorities and that it lowered Sufi standards to accommodate itself to Beduin laxity in religious matters. Yet the Grand Sanusi himself was a townsman, more at home in the schools and libraries of Fes, Cairo and Mecca than amid the rolling plains and plateaux of Cyrenaica where Beduin tribes pitched their camps and herded their animals. Even after founding the Mother Lodge of the Order on the Central Cyrenaican plateau in 1843, while the Sanusiya movement was still young in the country, the Grand Sanusi returned to Mecca for more than ten years. Altogether he spent only some ten years of his teaching life in Cyrenaica.

The Grand Sanusi was nearing 70 years of age when he came again to Cyrenaica. Doubtless he felt that the last years of his life should be devoted to contemplation, prayer and study. But it may also be true that he wished to place a wide stretch of desert between himself and the Turkish authorities of the Ottoman Empire which then extended over these lands. As the Sanusiya movement grew, these authorities began to take an ever greater interest in it, and the Grand Sanusi went first to live on the southern edge of the plateau where he built a lodge, and afterwards at Jaghbub, an oasis much further south. This was to become the center of the Order and the seat of an Islamic university.

In Jaghbub the Grand Sanusi set about building his headquarters, a large mass of stone buildings, some of them two-storied, enclosing a mosque and a school which were on an imposing scale for an oasis hitherto barely inhabited, a place of brackish water and small gardens. Around these central buildings and courts were built the houses of the Brothers of the Order, many of them teachers in the school, and houses for the students and for the Grand Sanusi's family. There were guest rooms,

The leader of the Sanusiya keeps his people pure in faith after they broke away from the rest of Islam to re-establish the true faith.

quarters for the slaves, kitchens and wells. The oasis was studded with date palms and just outside the main entrance to the village were irrigated gardens. The people now living there had no alternative but to use the brackish water for ordinary purposes; but fresh water for tea was obtained from infrequent showers which filled hollowed out cisterns in nearby rocks. The whole community at Jaghbub may have numbered round about 1,000 and as the oasis produced little apart from dates the supply problem must have been considerable. The community lived very largely on the goods sent there by the lodges of the Order elsewhere in Cyrenaica.

At Jaghbub, where the life of the community centered around the university, the Grand Sanusi, far from worldly distractions, was able to train the future leaders of the Order. The sheiks of the lodges of the Order were appointed by him from among his intimate circle of disciples, many of whom had followed him from afar on his travels. And in Cyrenaica he built a missionary organization which, with its focus in Jaghbub so distant from the Beduin tribal centers, prevented it from becoming identified with any one tribe or section of the country. It was the attachment of the tribes to their local lodges, and the attachment of the sheiks of these lodges to the Head of the Order in Jaghbub, which made the Order so effective as a missionary body and eventually enabled it to become a political force.

When the Grand Sanusi died in 1859, his two surviving sons were minors, so a regency of ten sheiks was appointed to conduct the affairs of the Order until the elder was old enough to take control. When he did so he dealt primarily with the general affairs of the Order, leaving the religious instruction in the hands of his brother. Under the leadership of the eldest son, Sayyid al-Mahdi, the Order expanded considerably, particularly among Beduin tribes of the Sahara and the Sudan. In its remarkable diffusion in north and central Africa, the Order never once resorted to the use of force to back its missionary labors. It is said of Sayyid al-Mahdi that the only instructions he gave his followers were to pray and obey God and His prophet; that he avoided making any show of his power and held himself apart from political questions. The Sanusiya Order co-operated with the Turks in the administration of Cyrenaica, although the Sanusi family and Brothers of the Order disapproved of their way of life. But the Order resisted Turkish demands for assistance in their war of 1876-8 against the Russians. The Order also refused the aid asked of it by Arabi Pasha in Egypt in 1882, and by the Sudanese Mahdi in 1883, against the British. Sayyid al-Mahdi rejected diplomatic overtures by the Italians and Germans, but when the French invaded the Order's Saharan territories and destroyed its religious houses, and when later the Italians did the same in Cyrenaica, the Order had no alternative but to resist. Yet although it was attacks from outside which destroyed the theocratic empire of the Sanusiya, it is doubtful whether such extensive territories could have been maintained anyway under single direction. The economic and political organization of the Order was crude even when elaborated in response to increasing trading activities and the need for maintaining peace in the petty and barbarous states which had come under its control. After Sayyid al-Mahdi's death, personal rivalries within the Sanusi family began to appear. It might indeed be said that it was only the Italian occupation of Libya in 1911 which outraged the Beduin tribesmen to such a degree that they rallied to the Order as a symbol of their common resistance.

In the time of Sayyid al-Mahdi the administration of the Order was simple in the extreme. Each lodge of the Order lived on its own revenues, derived from endowments, tithes, contributions of money, goods and transport. Each sent its surplus to Jaghbub or Kufra (where the leader had established himself) for the support of the university and the Sanusi family, and the general purposes of the Order. The sheik of each lodge arbitrated in disputes and wielded spiritual sanctions which compelled acceptance of his awards. There was, however, so little centralized planning that new lodges were sometimes founded on the initiative of influential families without the head of the Order hearing of the new foundation until its completion. In distant parts, the lodges were largely autonomous or came under the control of the local Mother Lodge. Yet as the combination of outside forces and administrative difficulties bore down on the Sanusiya Order, its realm was not totally destroyed. In Cyrenaica it remained strong and unified, even to the present day, although its political significance has been diminished in the modern state of Libya.

The rudiments of Islam which the Grand Sanusi found in the Beduin tribes of Cyrenaica made his teachings acceptable; the organization of the tribes made his Order possible as long as its focus was not associated with any single tribe or section of the country. But along with these factors must be accounted the way the lodges of the Order were compatible with the life of the Beduin tribespeople. The Sanusiya Order was always based on the tribes and never on the towns. The lodges were founded by the tribes or tribal sections who regarded them as tribal institutions. The tribal system and the Sanusiya organisation interpenetrated. It was this combination, allowing both for tribal allegiances and rivalries, which provided the Order with such sure foundations. Most tribal lodges were founded in a similar manner and seem to reflect tribal segmentation, mirroring lines of cleavage between tribes and tribal sections.

A tribe or section of a tribe saw with envy that a neighboring tribe had a lodge. They then sent a deputation to the head of the Order and asked him for a sheik to teach their children, cater for their religious needs, settle their disputes and so forth. The head of the Order granted them their request and sent them a sheik chosen from among the learned and pious men who surrounded him. The sheik probably took with him one or two companions, Brothers of the Order, to help him start the new lodge which the tribesmen built in the most favored part of their territory. Although they were simple structures they would often take many years to complete – and would be added to when further accommodation was required – in the leisurely Arab way. Most were built on Graeco-Roman foundations so that the tribesmen found stone ready to hand.

Some of the Cyrenaican lodges were larger than others but most were built with the same features: a straggling warren of stone buildings, comprising a mosque, schoolrooms, guest-rooms, apartments for the sheik and his family, rooms for teachers and pupils, houses for the Brothers, clients, servants and their families. Many had small gardens attached to them, just as at Jaghbub and, although few housed more than 50 or 100 people, their importance was measured by their tribal position and the number of their Beduin adherents.

The sheik of the new lodge would point out to the local tribesmen that he and his companions had no means of supporting themselves or of maintaining the lodge. The various tribal sections nearby then gave to the lodge lands adjoining it. This estate surrounding the lodge was known as its *haram*. On the Cyrenaican plateau the lodges were generously endowed with arable land, in the steppe with wells, and in the oases with date-palms and springs. Later further gifts of land, wells or palms would sometimes be made. A lodge might also obtain rights to land by asking permission of its owners to sow it. Constant repetition of this favor eventually gave the lodge rights for use in posterity.

The Beduin tribesmen also assisted the sheik of the lodge in the cultivation of the lands. At sowing time the sheik would pitch his tent near the area to be cultivated and prepare a communal meal, taking with him sacks of rice for the purpose. The local Beduin then came with their draft animals and sowed and plowed for a couple of days on behalf of the lodge. The same procedure took place at harvest time. And then besides these gifts of land and help in cultivation, the Beduin were expected to pay a tithe to the lodge at harvest time and after lambing. No doubt many of them paid annual dues, but this could not be enforced should they be averse to paying them.

The estates of the Sanusiya Order were inalienable endowments made in the love of God by tribal sections and sometimes by individuals. They belonged to the various lodges to which they were donated, with the Order as a whole as residuary, and not to the family of the Sanusi or the sheiks of the lodges. It was understood that when Beduin donated tracts of land, they could continue to pasture and sow on any parts not being used by the lodge. The revenues of one lodge could not be used to support another, and any surplus over the expenses of a lodge was paid into a central pool. Supplies sent to Jaghbub and Kufra by caravan included skins, wool, grain, butter, honey and meat; rice, tea, sugar, cloth and money were also sent. These were freewill gifts, though if a lodge did not send them, its sheik was reminded of his obligation. And this practice worked well enough during the lifetime of the Grand Sanusi and his sons. But as so often happens in Islamic orders, later descendants began to demand shares in the wealth of the Order.

In Cyrenaica, the endowments of the Order ran into many thousands of acres. The 14 lodges whose lands were technically registered in 1919 by an Italo-Sanusi commission possessed more than 100,000 acres. The total lands of the Order may well have been more than half a million acres. Much of the land was of use only for grazing, but much was agricultural land on the plateau. Wherever there were springs and gardens, there were properties of the Order, for such sites were suitable for the settlements of the Brothers since they, unlike the Beduin, were sedentary and house-dwellers. In the semi-desert lands, the Order owned or part-owned many of the best wells. Lodges were established on important caravan routes, on small inlets to command coastal trade, and in strong defensive positions. As already mentioned, many were built on Graeco-Roman sites, thus where Greeks, Romans or Turks found it convenient (or essential) to build villages and posts was also where the Sanusiya Order established its lodges. Anyone who observes the siting of the lodges will find them where one would expect them to be placed on a politico-economic plan. Just as the religion of the Grand Sanusi went to the very bones of the Beduin, so his Order established itself in the very arteries of Cyrenaica.

The Beduin are hard-headed people and they expect a return for their labor and gifts. The neighboring tribesmen considered that they were adequately rewarded for their support of the Sanusi lodges by the services the lodges rendered – for, like the Christian monasteries of Europe in the Dark Ages, Sanusiya lodges catered for more than just religious needs. They were schools, caravanserais, commercial centers, social centers, forts, courts of law, banks, store houses, poor houses, sanctuaries and burial grounds besides being channels through which ran a generous stream of God's blessing. They were centers of culture and security in a wild country and amid a fierce people. And they were stable points in a land where everyone was on the move; a Beduin camp might be anywhere. A Sanusiya lodge was fixed to the earth and its community with it. But the chief benefit of the lodges was, as the Grand Sanusi had told the Beduin long before, that they and their children might learn from scholarly and pious men the faith and precepts of Islam, that they might have the opportunity to worship in a mosque, and that by charity to their lodges they might earn recompense hereafter.

Glossary to the peoples of the Arab world

'Arab' was originally the name of the Semitic inhabitants of the Arabian peninsula. After the death of Mohammed and the birth of Islam as a fighting missionary religion, great migrations occurred and Arabs have spread out to cover most of the Middle East and North Africa. Today the word 'Arab' has come to mean generally all persons whose native language is Arabic, and who share a certain heritage and culture. Islam cannot be added to the definition, as there are many Christian Arabs and even Christian Arab communities as in the Lebanon. However, the vast majority of Arabs are Muslim. About one-tenth of the Arabs are Beduin nomads who traditionally despise agriculture. Most of these wander in the arid desert areas of Arabia and the Sahara with camels, goats and sheep or cattle. Most Arabs, however, are settled either in villages or towns. 30 million Arabs live in Egypt, 14 million in the Sudan, 13·5 million in Morocco, 12 million in Algiers, 8·2 million in Iraq, 8 million in Saudi Arabia, 5 million in Syria, 5 million in the Yemen, 4·5 million in Tunisia, 2·5 million in the Lebanon, 2 million in Jordan, 1·7 million in Libya and 0·5 million in Kuwait. Altogether there are nearly 107 million Arabs. Arabs are caucasoid people, but long periods of negro slavery among the tribes has left marked traces in the physical types. The largest minority among the Arabs are the Berber-speaking people of North Africa who lived there before the Arabs arrived.

In the Arab world a few small minorities, like the Copts, have retained their Christianity. Other minorities are recent arrivals who came and settled in countries who were already fully 'Arab': Armenians came from Anatolia in 1915, Circassians came from the Black Sea and Turkey, Kurds came from Turkey and Iran and the Turkomen from northern Turkey and Russia. Indians and Pakistanis live in fairly large numbers in the Trucial States and in the Sultanate of Oman. Many French and Spanish still live in once-occupied North Africa. Jews from all over the world have settled in Israel.

ABABDA see BEJA

ADIGHE see CIRCASSIAN

AGHBAR see SHLUH

AHAGGAREN see TUAREG (pages 92-101)

AL-KOWASIM *Population:* 20,000. Language: Arabic. Al-Kowasim are a powerful Maadic tribe who live in the sea ports of the 'Pirate Coast' (of the Persian Gulf). Today they are mainly fishermen, but in the past they were notorious pirates, especially between 1770 and 1820. At that period they operated in the Indian Ocean. Al-Kowasim are Sunni Muslim.

AMAMER see BEJA

ANAZAH *Population:* 50,000. Language: Arabic. The Anazah live in Nejd and the northern province of Saudi Arabia. Like most other nomadic tribes, Anazah live within well-defined grazing territories, and their lives are regulated by the seasons, the climate and the needs of their camels and other livestock. In summer they must camp near permanent waterholes, oases and villages. This is the time when they sell livestock to buy foods and manufactured goods, go to visit friends, and pay their taxes to the sheik. Just before the first rains fall, the camping units slowly move out into the desert. They keep an alert lookout for thunderstorms which bring much needed water. They travel from one pasture to another, often splitting into smaller groups, even single families. Towards spring they begin to come together again and regroup around the water holes, completing the cycle. The basic unit of the Anazah, as it is of most camel nomad tribes of Arabia, is the *hamulah* (womb) consisting of several related extended families. The head of the tribe is the paramount sheik who owes allegiance to the king only. Kinship is a most important factor, and Anazah, like other tribes, maintain that they are all the descendants of one illustrious male ancestor whose name they bear. The leader, or sheik, is selected from among the adult male members of one specific section of the lineage and need not necessarily be the son of the last sheik. He heads the council, *majlis*, of representative males which settles all the tribe's problems and disputes. There is no internal social stratification among the Anazah, as among other nomadic tribes of Arabia, but the tribe as a whole considers itself noble, and superior to the others, with some of whom they have long hereditary feuds.

ANTESSAR see TUAREG (pages 92-101)

ASSYRIAN *Population:* 40,000. Language group: Syriac, giving way to Arabic. The Assyrians live in central Iraq, in Kirkuk and Mosul. They are adherents of the ancient Nestorian 'Church of the East' which once flourished in Mesapotamia and carried on vigorous missionary activity from central Asia to China until the Mongol conquests in the 13th century. They are now scattered throughout the Middle East. Today most of the Assyrians in Iraq are employed in the oil fields. The titular head of the Assyrians is the Patriarch of the East who now lives in the US. The Assyrians are reputed to be brave and resourceful as well as technologically apt. Many Assyrians live in the Soviet Armenian Republic and in Iran.

AULLIMINDEN see TUAREG (pages 92-101)

AWAMIR *Population:* 1,400. Language: Arabic. The Awamir are divided into nomads and settled villagers. The nomads, who are the majority, roam the Arabian desert as far as Dhofar. The sedentary minority occupies a group of twelve villages near Nazwa in Oman. The nomad Awamir have a traditional feud with the Jenebeh tribe.

AWAZIM *Population:* unknown. Language: Arabic. The Awazim live in the eastern province of Saudi Arabia. Some raise sheep and others raise camels. They are considered ignoble and are looked down upon by the camel nomads, such as Anazah (q.v.). Many shepherds of the lowly *shwayah* group travel with the Awazim, caring for their own livestock and that of their Awazim masters. These have taken the tribal name Awazim and have become a part of the tribe.

BABAN see KURDS

BADINAN see KURDS

BAGGARA *Population:* 600,000. Language: Arabic. The Baggara live in the belt of savanna between Lake Chad and the White Nile in south-east Kordofan province, in the Sudan. The name Baggara means 'cattlemen', which they are as their land is too wet and muddy for the camel. Their staple foods are milk and its products, supplemented by bullrush millet which they have learned to cultivate without much enthusiasm. They keep sheep and goats and chickens for meat, but never slaughter a cow for food. The Baggara depend on barter for their grain, cloth and manufactured goods. They move with their livestock in regular cycles according to the seasons of the year. Their tents are light and simple, locally made (often from cattle hides) and cheaply replaced. Their only luxury items are the pieces of jewelry worn by the women. Baggara women enjoy more freedom than those of many other tribes.

BEDUIN *Population:* about 10 million. Language: Arabic. The Beduin are the nomadic tribesmen of the middle eastern deserts. About 10 per cent of the entire population of the area, they wander around almost 90 per cent of the land. The Beduin travel with their livestock, wandering in the deserts during the rainy season and settling around water sources for the dry summer season. They live in black goat-hair tents and subsist on the products of animal husbandry. Most prestigious among the Beduin are the camel nomads who wander in the Syrian and Arabian deserts and also in the Sahara (see Tuareg, pages 92-101). Beneath them rank the sheep and goat nomads who wander within the countries of the fertile crescent: Syria, Jordan, Iraq and Israel. Cattle nomads live mainly in south Arabia and in the Sudan (see Baggara). The Beduin are strongly patriarchal and tribal in character. The accepted way of living is in extended families in which each male has as many wives up to 4 as he can afford. Self-government within extended families and tribes is based on male heads of families. Religious traditions are very important to them, as are such values as hospitality, bravery, generosity, dignity and honor, vengeance and forgiveness, independence and leisure. Although the Beduin traditionally despise agriculture, they have in recent years become more settled as a result of centralization policies of the countries on whose lands they roam.

BEJA *Population:* 800,000. Language group: Hamitic, northern Cushitic branch. The Beja, who incorporate the Ababda, Beni Amer, Bisharin, Bogo, Hadendoa (q.v.) and Tigre tribes, inhabit the area between the Nile and the Red Sea and between the Egyptian border and the junction of the Atbara river and the Nile in northern Sudan. They first appear in Egyptian history in 2700 BC, when they already led their independent pastoral existence. They accepted Christianity in 600 AD, but were converted to Islam in 1300 AD and remain Muslim today. The Beja have copper-red to deep brown skin, moderate stature and wavy hair. They raise a little dura grain and subsist mainly on milk, butter and meat from sheep and goats, supplemented by cattle in the south and camels in the north. The Beja wander in small bands and camp in rectangular tents which have a framework of poles covered by grass and palm-leaf mats. Beja affairs are handled by a council of heads of families, and there is also a chief who has limited authority. They practise both circumcision and clitoridectomy. Where possible they follow the Muslim tradition of marriage with a father's brother's daughter, and pay a substantial bride-price. Polygyny is practised, but it is rare.

BENI AMER see BEJA

BENI BU HASSAN *Population:* 10,000. Language: Arabic. The people of Beni Bu Hassan live in Jaalan, in Oman. They follow the Ibadhi sect of Islam. Around their chief town, Belad Beni Bu Hassan, they cultivate dates and grain. They have few camels of their own, and must borrow more when going to war. The leadership is in the hands of three sheiks rather than one.

BENI GHAFIR *Population:* 5,000. Language: Arabic. The people of Beni Ghafir occupy the great valley which is named after them, and the localities of Bahila, Aridh, al-Dereez, al-Ghabbi and al-Ainan in Saudi Arabia. They are partly Sunni and partly Ibadhi Muslims. The men of Beni Ghafir have a reputation for valor in their frequent feuds with many of their neighboring tribes.

BENI YAS *Population:* 15,000. Language: Arabic. The people of Beni Yas have only recently settled in Oman. They now live in the towns of Abu Thubi and Debaje on the Trucial States coast, where they engage mainly in pearl fishing. Of both Beduin and Hadhr stock, they emigrated from Nejd around the middle of the 18th century after they gave up piracy.

BERABER *Population:* 450,000. Language group: Berber. The Beraber live in the Middle Atlas mountains of North Africa. They include the Idrassen, Nadhir, Seri, Serruchen, Sokhnon, Yafelman, Yussi, Zaer, Zayan, Zemmun and other tribes. Their main staples are barley and wheat, supplemented by maize, millet and sorghum. They keep sheep and goats and some other domestic animals, as beasts of burden and draft animals as well as for meat, hides, wools, milk and other dairy products. The majority of Beraber live in permanent dwellings all year round, while a minority accompany the flocks to the mountains in summer and the plains in winter. The extended family occupies a cluster of adjacent dwellings within compact and fortified settlements. They prefer rectangular houses with flat roofs, stone walls and no inner courtyard. Only the wealthy members of the Beraber tribes practise polygyny. They are all Muslim.

BERBER *Population:* about 10 million. Language: Berber. The Berber (see also Beraber, Shluh, Rif, Djerba) are the original inhabitants of North Africa. They live in a large number of pockets stretching from the western desert of Egypt to the Atlantic. In appearance the Berber resemble southern Europeans more than they do their Arab neighbors. All Berber are Muslim.
(pages 108-117)

BISHARIN see BEJA

BLAWA see SHLUH

BOGO see BEJA

CHERKESS see CIRCASSIAN

CIRCASSIAN *Population:* about 80,000, 12,000 of whom live in Jordan. Language group: Arabic. Most Circassian live in the north-west Caucasus near the Black Sea and in northern Turkey. There they are also known as Cherkess and differ from other tribes of the Caucasus in origin and language. In Jordan they call themselves Adighe, to avoid using Cherkess which is of Russian origin. In the past they had a unique form of government and a feudal system with princes, nobles and peasant classes who frequently fought one another. There was complete freedom of expression on matters of war and peace, and justice was administered by the old and respected of each tribe. The Circassians are nominally Muslim, but they retain many of their former pre-Islamic beliefs: the ancient gods Shible, of thunder, war and peace: Tleps, of fire: and Seosseres, of water and winds. There is a bride-price. Polygyny is forbidden and age is greatly respected. The Circassians live mainly off their herds of sheep and cattle but some have become town-dwellers and acquired various professions. Until recently Circassians still wore cossack-style clothes.

COPTS *Population:* 1 million. Language group: formerly Coptic, now Arabic. The Copts were the early native Christians of Egypt. They were converted as early as 250 AD, but only acquired their name in the 13th century. The clear Christian doctrine of life after death greatly appealed to the poorer people in Egypt, while it was scorned by the nobility. The Coptic church has traditionally been subject to both inner strife and corruption and to Muslim persecution which at times included wearing a compulsory heavy cross. More recently the Copts have been replaced as artisans and semi-skilled laborers by alien immigrants, and in the lower ranks of the Egyptian civil service by other Egyptians.

DADES see DRA'A

DJERBA *Population:* 40,000. Language group: Berber. The Djerba live on the island of Djerba, south-east Tunisia. They are sedentary cultivators of cereals and fruit. The Djerba belong to the Ibadite sect of Islam. In addition to their agriculture and raising herds of domestic animals, fishing is an important economic activity. They practise polygyny, favor marriage between first cousins and fatten the bride up for her wedding. Being an island people, Djerba have no need for the fortified dwellings which almost all the other Berber (q.v.) tribes live in. Their houses are rectangular, with flat terraced roofs, interior courtyards and thick external walls of stone or sun-dried brick.

DRA'A *Population:* 150,000. Language group: Berber. The Dra'a live in walled towns along the Dra river and its tributaries in southern Morocco. They include the Dades, Mesgita and Seddrat as well as the detribalized residents of Fezwala, Ktawa, Mhammid, Ternata and Tinzulin. They are all sedentary cultivators growing dates, and they supplement their diet by fishing. The Dra'a are nominally governed by a senate and an assembly, but often a few rich and powerful families take over, leaving the formal bodies police functions only. They often fight and feud among themselves. All Dra'a are Muslim.

DRUZES (see pages 84-85)

FELLAHIN *Population:* over 20 million. Language: Arabic. The Fellahin are the agriculturists of Egypt, living along the Nile valley and in its delta. They are of moderate stature, with a long and narrow head, broad face, strong jaws, prominent chin and full lips. Their skin color is light and their hair black and straight or wavy.
(see pages 60-79)

FILALA *Population:* over 100,000. Language group: Berber. The Filala live in the desert oases of Fenkla, Gheris, Tafilalet and Togda in south-east Morocco. They occupy several walled towns, and raise dates and other crops. All Filala are Muslim. Unlike the oasis-dwelling tribes, who are relatively egalitarian, the Filala have subjugated negro peoples of the area and have evolved a rigid system of social stratification. They are governed by two bodies: a senate and an assembly; the former dealing with external and the latter with internal affairs.

FRUGA see SHLUH

GEDMIRA see SHLUH

GHOMARA see SHLUH

GONTAFA see SHLUH

GREEK CYPRIOTS *Population:* 492,000. Language: Greek. Over three-quarters of the population of Cyprus are Greeks. There are deep-seated divisions between them and the Turkish Cypriot (q.v.) section of the population, chiefly based on their respective intense loyalty to, and identity with, Greek or Turkish culture. The appearance of Archbishop Makarios III in 1950 as a political spokesman for all Greek Cypriots gave a renewed emphasis to their ethnic identity. There are now very few mixed Turkish and Greek villages. Greeks are involved in most of the government and administrative work in the island and many of them work in industry, especially the profitable tourist industry. But Greek Cypriot life is based on the small farming villages in the dry lowland areas, where the houses are built of sun-dried mud bricks or stones. The Greeks' main foods are cheese made from goat's milk, kebab and moussaka, while the national drink is Turkish coffee. Their values are based on *philotimo,* a concept of honor, based on individualism and family loyalty. They are Christians of the Eastern Orthodox Church.

HADENDOA *Population:* unknown. Language group: Hamitic. The Hadendoa live in the country south and east of Bisharin Territory along the Khor Baraka river. They are members of the large Beja (q.v.) group of tribes, but are taller and often darker than other Beja peoples. They are fervently Muslim.

HAHA see SHLUH

HAWARA see SHLUH

HUTAYM *Population:* 40,000. Language: Arabic. The Hutaym live scattered throughout northern Nejd in Saudi Arabia. They are mainly artisans who wander the desert or attach themselves to the nobler camel nomad tribes and serve them. They are Muslim.

IDRASSEN see BERABER

IFORA see TUAREG (pages 92-101)

IHAJENEN see TUAREG (pages 92-101)

JERRAR see SHLUH

JEWS *Population:* over 2·5 million. Languages: Hebrew, Arabic and European languages according to country of origin. Most of the Jews in the Arab world now live in the State of Israel. Many have come there as refugees from eastern and central Europe after World War II, mainly from Poland, Hungary and the Baltic countries. Others arrived from all over the world after the Jewish state was established in 1948. 700,000 have emigrated from Arab countries, mainly Morocco (275,000), Iraq (126,000) and Algeria (128,600). Their history in the Arab countries has been one of second class citizenship and occasional persecutions. 60,000 of them still live in Arab countries: 35,000 in Morocco, 9,000 in Tunisia, 2,000 in the Lebanon, 2,000 in Syria and a few hundred in Iraq where they fare badly. The Jewish communities of Libya and the Yemen, who once numbered about 50,000 each, no longer exist as a result of mass immigration mainly to Israel.
(see pages 38-49)

KABABISH *Population:* 70,000. Language: Arabic. The Kababish live in the northern Kordofan province of Sudan. During the 19th century Kababish carried trade goods between the Nile and Dafrur province, and also imposed taxes on caravans. Then, as now, they were mainly camel nomads, and also kept other livestock. They have a regular cycle of travel with their animals, according to the seasons of the year, and cultivate very little. All Kababish are Muslim, and 99 per cent are illiterate.

KABYLE *Population:* 1 million. Language group: Berber. The Kabyle are sedentary cultivators living in a coastal region of Algeria. Grain, figs and olives are the staples of Kabyle diet. They are one of the few Berber tribes whose men have more than one wife if they can afford the bride-price. Extended families occupy a single compound within the settlement. They live in rectangular houses with gable roofs covered with tiles. All Kabyle are Muslim. The traditional attire for men is the *gandurah,* a loose flowing garment worn with a black and white woolen skullcap and a broad-brimmed straw hat. The women wear bright yellow garments with stripes, silk scarves and heavy silver jewelry. Each Kabyle village is administered by an assembly of men working according to a set code of laws. They have a system of social stratification with out-caste smiths and butchers at the bottom of the scale.

KARAITE *Population:* 10,000. Language: Hebrew. The Karaite sect was founded in 760 AD by Anan Ben David of Baghdad, as an anti-Rabbinic religious innovation prompted by political motivation. The Karaites reject the Oral Jewish laws, accept only the Scriptures themselves and differ from the Jews in matters like the calender, observance of the Sabbath and religious laws. Intermarriage with Jews is therefore impossible. Today the Karaites live in and around the town of Ramla, not far from Tel-Aviv, Israel. They have nine synagogues of their own, each with its minister-reader.

KSIMA see SHLUH

KURDS *Population:* 5·5 million (800,000 in Iraq). Language group: Indo-European, Kurdish. The vast majority of Kurds live around the frontiers of Turkey, Iran and Iraq. In Iraq most Kurds, apart from the few who have drifted to the cities, live in isolated villages in the mountain valleys of the Turkish and Iranian border areas. The provinces of Mosul, Irbil, Kirkuk and Diyala are heavily Kurdish and Sulaymaniyah is almost exclusively so. The Kurd is a hardy mountain warrior, taller and more strongly built than the Arab *fellah*, devoted to his upland farm and pastures and fiercely resentful of his political subordination to the Arab ruling groups. The majority have for some time been cereal farmers and stock-breeders who travel with their flocks according to the seasons of the year. Only a few are still fully nomadic. The Kurds are divided into three main groups: Badinan are an extension of the Turkish Kurds and speak Kermanji or 'literary Kurdish'. Suran and Baban speak the same dialect of Kurdish and consist of nomadic tribes, freehold farmers and detribalized tenant farmers and laborers. Nowadays many Kurds speak Arabic as well, and are finding it easier to forget their traditional clannishness and rigid ways through the Sunni Muslim faith that they share with their Arab neighbors. However Kurdish nationalism is still a strong political factor in Iraqi life.

LUR *Population:* 2 million, 60,000 in Iraq. Language: dialect of Persian. Most Lur live in Iran. The Lur who live in the eastern part of Iraq entered many generations ago over the Pusht i Kuh mountains, and now form a large part of the population of Badrah and Mandali. They are more often town or village laborers than agriculturalists, and often take jobs as heavy porters in the big cities. They are Shi'ite Muslim, but demonstrated little political consciousness, in spite of the fact that the Kurds (q.v.) would like their support for a proposed Kurdish State.

MANDAEAN see SABAEAN

MARONITES *Population:* over 1 million in the Lebanon, 3,000 in Cyprus. Language: Arabic and Greek. The Maronites are Christians who belong to one of the Eastern branches of the Roman Catholic church, which traces its origin to Saint Maron, a 5th century hermit who lived and taught in the Lebanon. In that country they are the majority of the Christian community, which shares political power equally with the Muslim community. In Cyprus they are farmers and traders, hardly distinguishable from the Greek Cypriots (q.v.).

MARSH ARABS (pages 28-29)

MASSAT see SHLUH

MAURI see MOOR

MAURITANIAN see MOOR

MELALSA see RIF

MENABA see SHLUH

MENTAGA see SHLUH

MESGINA see SHLUH

MESGITA see DRA'A

MOOR *Population:* about 1 million. Language: Arabic. The Moors, also known as Mauri and Mauritanians, are the inhabitants of the area which lies between the south of Morocco and the republics of Senegal and Mali. Most of this area is now the Islamic Republic of Mauritania. The Moors of Mauritania are nomads. Their livestock consists mainly of cattle of the Maure type, but there are sheep and goat nomads along the coasts. They use camels throughout as draft animals. The export of gum arabic was once economically important, but is now less so. In English literature the word 'Moor' has been used to mean different things: often it has meant the equivalent of 'Moroccan'; it has been used to describe the former Muslims of Spain, of mixed Arab, Spanish and Berber origins who created the Arab Andalusian civilization and settled in northern Africa between the 11th and 17th centuries; it is sometimes used as a substitute for Muslim.

MTUGA see SHLUH

NADHIR see BERABER

NTIFA see SHLUH

NUBIAN *Population:* 1 million. Language group: Kenuzi and Mahasi, with Arabic. The Nubians of Egypt (200,000) once lived in the upper reaches of the Nile valley. They had to leave when the High Dam of Aswan was built, and were deprived of their livelihoods. Many were resettled, others went into domestic service in Egyptian cities, where they gained an excellent reputation for their cleanliness, intelligence and honesty. Other Nubians now live south of the dam and railhead at Aswan, and beyond in northern Sudan. They are taller and darker than the Egyptians.

PALESTINIAN *Population:* over 1·5 million. Language: Arabic. Palestinians live scattered all over the Middle East; many of them have emigrated to Europe and the Americas. The Palestinians are normally considered to be Arabs who lived within the borders of Mandatory Palestine, between the Mediterranean Sea and the River Jordan, before 1948. At that time the Palestinians were the most literate of Arabs and many played important roles in governing the country. A high proportion of them lived in towns. Following the partition of Palestine by the UN, the declaration of the State of Israel and the war of 1948 about 450,000 Palestinians left or were driven out of the 'Jewish sector'. These are the Palestinians who have been refugees for over 25 years. Half a million or more Palestinians came, at the same time, under Jordanian rule on the west bank of the Jordan which was occupied by Israel in 1967. Jordan was the only Arab state to grant citizenship to the Palestinians, and there are about a million of them living within her borders. Nearly a quarter of these live in refugee camps, and a quarter more hold refugee cards. There are about 250,000 Palestinian refugees living in camps in the Gaza Strip (also under Israeli occupation since 1967), about 120,000 in Lebanon (but only about 80,000 in camps, mostly in the south) and about 100,000 in Syria. About 400,000 Arabs live in Israel itself, including 30,000 Druzes and many Beduin; not all of these choose to describe themselves as Palestinians, a term which has come to have deep political significance. Many of them have been assimilated in varying degrees into the countries where they have been living since 1948, but there is a strong nationalistic movement which has in recent years become highly militant. Most Palestinians are Sunni Muslim. About 12 per cent are Christian.

QURAISH *Population:* unknown. Language: Arabic. Quraish is the tribe of Mohammed and the early caliphs. Today, however, the tribe survives only as two weak groups of sheep herders, one near at-Faif, the other near Jabal Arafat, in Saudi Arabia.

RIF *Population:* 700,000. Language group: Berber. The Rif include the Melalsa, Znassen, Ghomara, Riffian and Senhaja nations, occupying the mountainous Rif region of northern Morocco. Their main subsistence is cereal agriculture but they also fish, mainly for sardines. They are cattle breeders and also have sheep and goats. A Rif who can afford to may marry more than one wife. Cousins may marry, but a man is forbidden to wed his father's brother's daughter, who would be his ideal bride according to the Arabs. The extended family live together in a cluster of dwellings. The Rif have a rigid class system which includes out-castes such as smiths, musicians and town criers. They live in rectangular houses with flat terraced roofs and interior courtyards, the gable roofs covered with shingles. The Rif are the fairest of all Berber tribes and have a reputation for being great warriors. They are all Sunni Muslims.

SABAEAN *Population:* 7,000. Language: Arabic. The Sabaean (or Mandaean) are an urban-dwelling group, scattered among the towns along the rivers south of Baghdad, Iraq. They are generally thought to be diminishing in numbers; the popular explanation is the reputed beauty of their women who are much sought as wives by men of other groups. The Sabaean are an industrious and peaceable people, and are required by their religion to live near running water to perform numerous ablutions. Therefore one of their principal traditional occupations has been boat-building. They also enjoy a high local reputation as silversmiths, specializing in Amarah-work of antimony designs on silver.

SAMARITANS *Population:* 400. Language: Hebrew and Arabic. 150 Samaritans live in Israel in the town of Holon and 250 in Nablus. In Holon they have a synagogue; their high priest lives in Nablus, and several families live on Mount Grizim which is sacred to them. On the Mount they celebrate the Passover traditionally, including the ritual sacrifice of sheep. The Samaritans, who claim to be the descendants of the ten lost tribes of Israel, are not allowed to intermarry with Jews. Their small numbers and constant internal marriages have caused genetic defects to become more pronounced among them, and has increased their similarity to one another.

SEDDRAT see DRA'A

SEKSAWA see SHLUH

SEMLAL see SHLUH

SEMNEG see SHLUH

SENHAJA see RIF

SERI see BERABER

SERRUCHEN see BERABER

SHABAK *Population:* 12,000 in Iraq. Language group: Indo-European, Kurdish dialect. The Shabak live in agricultural villages on the Tigris, south of Mosul and in the Sinjar district, where they maintain close relationships with the neighboring Yezidi (q.v.), and also occupy a few villages on both banks of the Greater Zab. They are distinguished from the Kurds by their religious beliefs and observances which resemble those of the Ali ilahi Shi'ite sect, but are peculiar in respect to certain secret rites.

SHAMMAR *Population:* unknown. Language: Arabic. The Shammar live in the northern part of Nejd province in Saudi Arabia. They are one of the most powerful tribes of the camel nomads. Their traditional way of life closely resembles that of the Anazah (q.v.).

SHLUH *Population:* over 1 million. Language group: Berber. The Shluh include the Aghbar, Blawa, Fruga, Gedmira, Gontafa, Haha, Hawara, Jerrar, Ksima, Massat, Menaba, Mentaga, Mesgina, Mtuga, Ntifa, Seksawa, Semlal, Semneg, Shtuka, and other tribes of the Grand Atlas, the Anti-Atlas, the valley of the Sous river and the adjacent coast of Morocco. They are mainly sedentary cereal cultivators, supplementing their diet with fishing. Marriage involves a bride-price; the Shluh are strictly monogamous. The mountain Shluh tend to be egalitarian, but the valley Shluh, who subjugated the local negro population, have developed a rigid class system. The Shluh have a complex system of local government based on units called *lef*, alliances that coordinate things like grazing rights in peacetime, but are also defensive in time of war. All Shluh are Muslim.

SHTUKA see SHLUH

SOKHNON see BERABER

TEDA (pages 80-83)

TIBU see TEDA (pages 80-83)

TIGRE see BEJA

TUAREG (pages 92-101)

TURKISH CYPRIOTS *Population:* 140,000. Language group: Turkic. The Turks in Cyprus are 18 per cent of the population. Most of the rest are Greek Cypriots (q.v.). They have strong cultural and religious ties with Turkey. Since violent clashes between Greeks and Turks in Cyprus in 1963, there are few mixed villages. They are farmers and some keep sheep and goats. Some of them are semi-nomadic herdsmen. An increasing number of young Turks now work in mining, manufacturing and public services. As a result of the troublès some Turks have become more isolated. Many are unemployed and forced to live in crowded conditions. All Turkish cypriots are Sunni Muslim. There are a further 300,000 Turks of Cypriot origin living in Turkey.

TURKOMEN *Population:* 1,500,000, 75,000 in Iraq. Language group: Turkic. Most Turkomen live in the Soviet Republic of Turkmenia. In Iraq the Turkomen live in northern Iraq in the areas of Qarah Tappah, Kirkuk, Irbil and Tal'Afar. The group as a whole, particularly the younger generation, is being assimilated in language and social patterns into the Arab population, except for the Jarjriyah Turkomen who retain tribal organization. As in Ottoman times, a much larger percentage of government functionaries are Turkomen than might be expected from their small numbers.

WARAIN *Population:* 100,000. Language group: Berber. The Warain are a semi-nomadic tribe living in the eastern part of the Middle Atlas mountains in Morocco. They cultivate cereals and have herds of sheep and goats. In their permanent settlements the houses are rectangular with thick walls, flat roofs and interior courtyards except for the northern Warain whose houses lack the courtyard. They have to some extent adopted the *lef* system of local government which is based on alliances that coordinate grazing rights in peace time and become defensive units at times of war.

YAFELMAN see BERABER

YEZIDI *Population:* 35,000 in Iraq. Language group: Indo-European (Kermanji). The official use of the term 'Yezidi' in Iraq is indicative of their status, for the word has a pejorative connotation; the name used by the people themselves is 'Dasnayi'. More concentrated than any other Iraqi minority, they are a majority in Sinjar, where they live in villages. They probably today represent a smaller proportion of the population than some hundred years ago, having been subjected to several decimating excursions by the Turkish authorities and their Kurdish neighbors in Ottoman times. Yezidi have traditionally been set apart from the mainstream of Iraqi life. They are execrated as 'devil worshippers' by the major Muslim sects, and their individual articles of faith make it difficult for them even to send their children to public schools. Despised by the majority and at the bottom of the economic scale, Yezidi have been able to participate in and enjoy Iraq's development less than any other people.

YUSSI see BERABER

ZAER see BERABER

ZEMMUN see BERABER

ZNASSEN see RIF

(All population figures are approximate)